Abiding In The Stillness

Abiding In The Stillness

Realising a Life of Abundance

by

Jim Fox

Published by
The Centre of the Labyrinth

First published and distributed in the United Kingdom by:
The Centre of the Labyrinth
The Centre, 1 Pell Street, Swansea, SA1 3ES
Tel.: (44) 1792 477123
www.thecentre-swansea.co.uk

A catalogue record for this book is available from the British Library

ISBN 978-0-9573855-2-8

**This book is dedicated to
my partner & soul mate
Kiera
&
to my wonderful daughters
Donna & Rhian**

CONTENTS

PART TWO - INSPIRATION

Introduction

You don't have to believe everything you read in this book!

Firstly I would ask you to read it, and then try it for yourself. Put it into practice, then, and only then, if it resonates with you and works for you, you can believe it.

It is not my intention to tell you what to do, but rather to encourage you to connect with the **Stillness** inside yourself and to listen to that divine voice which is in each and every one of us. You can call it god, spirit, source, the divine mind, divine energy, universe, goddess - whatever term you use it doesn't really matter, it all comes down to the same thing, that creative energy which is the basis of all that is. Throughout this book I will be using one or other of these terms, but to me they all mean and represent the same thing. I hope this doesn't confuse you, it's just that as yet nobody seems to have come up with a universal term for the universal energy. If we could have one word that describes it, that word might be love; but even then it doesn't really fully do it justice.

What does it mean to be Abiding in the Stillness?

In my previous book, *Be Still – Simple Keys to Living a Spiritual Life in a Material World,* we looked at the importance of being **Still** and how we can find that Stillness. In this book the emphasis is on abiding, or living in the stillness at all times, so that stillness is our home – our abode. When we can actually take up residence in a place of Stillness we find that our whole life changes. Our outlook changes, our attitude changes, our reactions to events and people changes. **Abiding in the Stillness** is a precious state that, once we have moved in and experienced it there is nothing that we would allow to take us away from that place. Just as we would protect our property from intruders and unwanted guests, we find that we have the same response to unwanted stress, aggravation, disturbance and other invasions that would take away our peace. We simply won't allow it in.

Realisation

Throughout my writings there is one word that seems to crop up more than any other - the word ***realise***. If you search a dictionary for the word *realise* you will find a number of different definitions, probably the most familiar to us is when we use it to describe that "*light-bulb*" moment when we become fully aware of something; to understand clearly. However, much of the time when I use the word, I am thinking of the other definitions you may find in the dictionary.

To cause to happen,

To fulfil,

To achieve,

To give form to.

Perhaps my favourite meaning is when it used to describe realising one's assets; the conversion of assets into hard cash. In the context of this book I am talking about converting knowledge of something, seen as an asset, into reality or "the hard cash", which enables you to use that knowledge and to live it, rather than keeping it filed away for a rainy day or for safe-keeping.

To **realise** means to **make real.**

As you read this book and you see the word **realise** in bold face, try to see its meaning in the fullness in which it is intended, and turn the understanding into reality.

It is my intention that you read this book in a place of Stillness, and that you allow the spirit within to show you what is truth. Then, you will know the truth and the truth will set you free.

Part One

Living In Abundance

1

AN ABUNDANT LIFE

It is an amazing privilege for me to be sharing with you what I believe to be some of the principles that lead to experiencing, and enjoying an abundant life. For many years I have believed that it is our right and destiny as human beings to live life to the full, to enjoy the limitless bounty that life and the universe has to offer. However, so many of us don't seem to be able to open the door to the storehouse of blessings that are just waiting there for us to claim them as our own. Health, wealth, happiness, contentment, security, love, fulfilment, they are all waiting for us to take hold of them and to claim them as our own.

Some people spend a lifetime searching for the key to life and very often their search ends in frustration and disappointment. A whole lifetime can be spent moving from one philosophy to another, one religion to another, one self-help guru to another, going from talk to talk, reading all the latest books and theories but still never actually finding the key that they are looking for to enable them to open the door that will lead them into fulfilment and abundance. Right from the outset I'm going to let you into a secret that you may not yet have discovered for yourself – **the door is not actually locked!**

That's right; the door to abundant life is open, and it always has been. It is only our thinking and conditioning that has led us to believe that the door is locked and we need to find a key. There is no lock on the door, we don't need to search for the key, the only thing that we have to do is to get up, go to the door and open it in order to claim what is ours by right.

The reality however, is that even though the door to the Storehouse of Abundance is not locked, we ourselves have become locked. We have become enchained in our mind, in our body and in our spirit. We have allowed ourselves through years of conditioning, religious teaching, philosophical argument, parental guidance, social laws and authoritarian dictate to believe that we are not worthy, or that we have to strive towards some sort of perfection or higher standing in order to free ourselves from the mundane, from the rut of life.

In the following pages I hope to be able to show you the keys that you can use in order to free yourself, that you might be able to enjoy an abundant life so that when the days of this incarnation come to an end you will know that you have experienced the fullness of life with all its blessings and joys.

2

WHAT IS ABUNDANCE?

In recent years there has been an abundance of books, DVDs & CDs on the subject of the Law of Attraction, and it is my guess that this may not be the first book that you have read that deals with how to enjoy abundance. One of my concerns about all the interest there has been is that very often no account is made for "responsibility". The responsibility that we hold in putting out the desires for what we want, or what we think we need.

It seems to me that it is very easy to slip into greed and shallowness. In this book we are going to look at the Holistic Approach to enjoying Abundant Life, which hopefully, will enable us to have a right and balanced attitude to the Law of Attraction, and to understand that abundance does not mean greed or having more than we can possibly need or use. I feel that much of the teachings and books that have been written on the subject of the Law of Attraction make it too simplistic and actually, unbalanced. It often seems a bit like putting the cart before the horse when we say that if you ask for something and then focus your attention on it, it will come to you.

My own belief and experience with the Law of Attraction is that if FIRST we learn to **Be Still** and make connection with the divine source within us, we will know which direction we are to travel in and what we need in order to make that journey. It is then that we can ask for what we need and, beyond any shadow of a doubt, those things that we need **will** come to us.

The Law of Attraction is not about asking for things that we want in order for us to have more, or better than we already have. It is about having what we need in order to fulfill our purpose, or dharma, in this life.

It is also my belief that everything and everyone in the universe is connected, that we are all part of the same whole. No one is truly independent. If I have accumulated great wealth and riches through my application of the law of attraction whilst my neighbour is in need, it is a bit like having an expensive jacket to wear whilst my trousers are in threads and I have holes in my shoes. Abundance is having enough to share with those who are in need, and then to share it with them.

I'm not only talking about material wealth and possessions here, abundance is part of what I would call the holistic life, or the whole life. So, when we talk about abundance we are talking about spiritual, mental and emotional abundance as well as physical and material abundance. If you have an abundance of spiritual knowledge and enlightenment, it is yours to share freely. If you have an abundance of mental wisdom or knowledge, or emotional strength, it is yours to share freely. Likewise, if you have a material abundance you have that as part of the universal whole in order to be able to share it freely. It is not about hoarding or storing up treasures on earth; it is about sharing those treasures that you have been blessed with for the greater good of the whole.

It is interesting to note that the word abundance comes from the Latin word meaning "to overflow". To be living in abundance means to be overflowing, to have more than you as a vessel can hold. If we allow that which overflows to simply be wasted, we are only adding to the need and suffering in the world around us, and if we are all connected in the universe then we are ultimately adding to our own need and suffering by allowing greed to dominate our lives. I have a picture in my mind's eye as I write this, of one of those champagne fountains, or waterfalls, that you sometimes see at weddings. As the glass at the top of the pyramid fills and overflows into the glasses immediately below, they then overflow into the next level and so on until dozens of glasses are all filled, all from the overflow of the one glass at the top. When we allow our abundance to overflow there is really no limit to the number of people who will also benefit from what we share.

*

With abundance also comes responsibility, and with responsibility comes an awareness of being part of the greater whole. We do not stand alone; we are inextricably linked with each other as one body in the universe. What affects me also affects you and what affects you affects me. We each have a responsibility to look after the whole in the same way that we have a responsibility to look after our own personal body. To neglect one part of the body means that the whole body does not function in the way that it should and if the body is not functioning correctly then it is not reaching its full potential and destiny. Look at any newspaper or news broadcast and you will hear of wars, murders, abuses, crimes, poverty, starvation etc. When we realise the fact that we are all part of the one whole we must also realise that each one of us is responsible for the way the world is today.

Living a fulfilled, abundant life is not just for the benefit of the individual but also for the benefit of the entire human race, and the whole universe of which we are all an important part.

When you **realise** that you have enough, you are truly rich.

I remember as a child in Sunday school singing the refrain:

"Count your blessings, name them one-by-one.

And it will surprise you what the lord has done"

Before you move on to the next chapter, why not take a pen and paper and start to make a list of all the good things, all the blessings, all that you have to be grateful for. When you think you have finished take some time to **Be Still** and listen to the spirit within, then go back to your list and add all the things that you have been reminded of in the Stillness. Did you remember such things as the electricity that powers all the things in your home? What about your shoes? What about the rain that helps the vegetables that are part of your diet, to grow? The more you are aware, the more you will be surprised at what blessings the universe provides for you. You may even be surprised to **realise** that you already have more than you need, that you are already living in abundance.

3

OWNING YOUR SELF

Right now I would like to encourage you to concentrate on where you are at this moment. You see, this moment is all that is actually important.

There is only one time and that time is Now.

It doesn't matter what has happened in the past. It doesn't matter what you have done or what you have been in the past. The past has gone, all that matters is **Now**.

It doesn't matter about what might happen in the future. It doesn't matter about what plans you might have for the future. The future is not here, all that matters is **Now**.

The past has gone – it will always be the past.

The future will always be the future – it never arrives.

It is always **Now**.

I have often heard Ram Dass say that there are two questions that no matter when we ask them of ourselves, the answer will always be the same.

"*Where am I?*" and "*What time is it?*"

Whenever and wherever you ask yourselves these two questions you can always reply with the same answers.

"*Where am I?*"

"Here"

"What time is it?"

"Now"

What matters is now - this moment. Right here, right now.

Why is this important? It's because so much of what we believe and feel now is influenced by the past. By what we have been told, and by the conditioning we have been subjected to as we were growing up. You believe you are not worthy because maybe you were told that you were a miserable sinner. You believe that you can never be a success because your teacher always put you down. You believe that you will never be wealthy because of your social background and upbringing, or maybe because you have been told so many times that wealth and riches are not for the likes of you and that you were not destined to have material success. You believe that you will never be liked because as a child you were picked on and bullied. You believe that you will always be second rate because your parents always compared you with an older brother or sister, saying, "*why can't you be like them?*" You believe you are not musical because you were told that you were singing out of tune in the school choir. Everything you believe about yourself is a result of what you have been told. It is time to put aside the things that you have been told and to start to live your own life, and to live it now.

You are not the same person that you were when you were 11. You are not the same person you were when you were 21. Whatever age you are now, you are not the same person that you were 7 or 8 years ago.

Did you know that different cell types have different lifespans? The cells that make up your skin and the cells in your mouth have a very fast rate of mitosis. The cells lining your stomach divide in order to replace the ones that are eaten away by stomach acid. Your bone marrow replenishes your red blood cells every 3 months. It is true that some of the cells that make up the nervous system never divide once they have formed. Recently however, nervous system stem cells have been discovered in an adult, providing evidence that some new nervous tissue cells are actually being made right into adulthood. There is not a consistent rate of replacement, your body doesn't completely replace itself, but certainly most of it does over varying periods of time. About 75% of your body is water and every month or so almost all the water in your body is replaced, about 7% of your body weight is blood fluid and blood cells, most of which are replaced in a three month period. So, on a physical level you are not the same as you were even three months ago. As we are constantly changing on a physical level, there is therefore no need to hang on to old belief systems, old conditioning, old negativity, old limitations, or even old illnesses. You are who you are now, at this moment - not who you used to be.

Not only are you perfectly you now, you are also unique – there is no one else in the world just like you, neither has there ever been anyone just like you. You are not like anyone else. You don't need to live your life in the way that somebody else wants you to. You don't need to try and be somebody else, no matter how great that person was. There was only one Francis of Assisi; you don't need to be another Francis. You don't need to be another Buddha, you don't need to be another Gandhi, you don't need to be another Churchill or Lloyd-George and, perhaps most importantly, you don't need to be your parents. You are you. Be yourself. Do you want to know how unique you actually are? Nobody, in the history of the human race has ever had, or ever will have the same fingerprints that you have, even if you happen to be an identical twin – there is only one you and there only ever will be one you.

It is time to stop trying to change who you are. Stop trying to change your self. Any change that needs to take place will happen naturally when you are living in holistic balance and harmony. When we **Abide in the Stillness** we don't allow ourselves to be affected by how other people see us or how other people think we should be. In the **Stillness** we accept ourselves as we are and for whom we are.

4

THE TRIPOD EFFECT

In order for us to experience and enjoy a full, or an abundant life, we need to realise that not only are we a part of the whole, but that we are ourselves a whole made up of many different parts. Whenever I am giving a talk on the subject of Stillness, I often begin by stating that I do not have a soul. I like to make it clear, right from the beginning, that I do not believe that I have a soul. I do believe however, that **I am** a soul and that I **have** a body. I usually get some strange and confused looks from this until the reality of what I am saying sinks in.

I love the energy and beneficial effects of singing and chanting mantras. One particular mantra that I enjoy and find really empowering, has the words *"Ma Dehane Me Atma Om"*, which means *"I am not the body, I am the soul"* By singing and repeating these words I am reminded that who or what I am is far greater than the physical, material me.

I believe that we are spiritual beings who have a physical body in which we dwell, and that we have a mind with which to think and to hold thoughts. My body is a vehicle that enables me to express myself without scaring the living daylights out of people. I'm sure that people find it much more acceptable and not so off-putting if I am able to appear in a physical form when speaking to them rather than them just hearing a strange disembodied voice! Just as I see my body as a vehicle, I consider my mind, or my intelligence, to be like a computer that enables me to respond and to articulate. My mind, if you like, is the receiver that picks up and translates all the thoughts that are floating around in the ether. Like a radio receiver, when it is tuned in to the correct frequency I am able to **realise** my connection with the divine mind of the universe.

Whilst the real me is the spiritual essence that dwells in the physical, I also believe that as our spirits or souls have chosen to be in this earthly incarnation, we must also be aware that our physical bodies and our minds are equally important. We have a duty, if you like, to see that there is balance between our body, mind and soul and to care for each aspect of our being.

The physical, mental and spiritual elements of our lives make up the whole that is our self. It is no good us being so spiritually minded that we are of no earthly use. It is no good us being so mentally aware and developed that we neglect the spiritual side of our life. It is no good us putting so much emphasis on the physical and material things of life that we fail to think and to use our minds in a balanced way. We live in a material world where we need to think and feel emotions and where we need to have awareness that life transcends the material and carries over into a spiritual dimension, not just when we die, but right here, right now at this present moment. We cannot get away from this reality and if we are to function properly and to enjoy the bounty and blessings that the universe has in store for us, we need to have these three areas in balance in our life.

I want you to imagine a camera tripod, or better still if you actually have one, go and get it and place a camera on it. Now, before you do anything with the tripod, I want you to draw three vertical lines on a sheet of paper and label these lines physical/material, mental/emotional, and spiritual. Starting from the top of each line, mark out 10 equal sections numbering them 1 to 10. Now, where 1 is the weakest at the top of the line and 10 is the strongest at the base of the line, I want you to mark on each one where you feel you are right now, in relation to the importance you give to each of these areas in your life. So if you feel that you maybe give more importance to your spiritual life at maybe 8 or 9, mark the line there. If you feel you don't give much importance to the material things of life, let's say 5 or 6, mark the line at this point. Perhaps you like to think and reason a lot and this is a fairly important area to you somewhere between 7 and 10, make a mark on the mental line there. Ok, now I want you to go back to the tripod and using 10 as fully extended on the legs and 1 as the minimum extension, I want you to identify each of the legs as you did the lines, and to adjust them accordingly.

You will probably now be looking at a tripod with 3 legs of different lengths. If you have been able to use your own tripod and you have the camera in place I'd like you to look through the viewfinder and see how the image is presented. This is representative of the way you are viewing the world around you from your state of imbalance. Take a photograph and keep it for future reference. When you have finished reading this book, try repeating this exercise and hopefully we will have come to a point when each of the legs is set at the same length and the image in the viewfinder will be balanced and stable.

Our aim now is to come to a point when we are giving balanced attention to Mind, Body & Spirit.

In the following chapters we are going to be looking at each of these three aspects of our lives to see where we might be going wrong and missing out, what we can do to redress the balance and how we can use this to experience and enjoy Abundant Life.

5

FINDING THE BALANCE – THE SPIRITUAL

Ideally, we would like all three of the legs on our tripod to be extended to the maximum possible length. This will not only give us balance but also ensure that we are reaching our true potential in this particular incarnation that we have chosen. I believe that it is totally possible to be reaching our full potential in the physical, mental and spiritual area of our lives, not settling for anything less than that which we are able to achieve. Now this doesn't mean that we are all meant to be Einsteins, Dalai Lamas or Usain Bolts, but we can all live up to our own individual potentiality.

Let's start by looking at the spiritual aspect of our lives, as I believe that this can provide a good solid foundation for all other areas of our being. If we can approach the material and emotional aspects of our lives from an open and balanced spiritual awareness, it enables us to see clearly and understand how we can bring harmony and balance into the whole that is our life.

It is important that we establish what I mean by spirituality and, perhaps even more importantly, what I don't mean. Let me make it perfectly clear that when I talk about spirituality I am not talking about religion in any form whatsoever. Spirituality and religion are two entirely different things. The word "*religion*" comes from the Latin words "*religio*" and "religare" meaning bond, or to bind, whereas spirituality is all about freedom. All the world's leading religions are supposedly based on the teachings of great teachers who themselves spoke out against religion. Jesus, Buddha, Mohammed, Krishna, all spoke about the futility of religion and emphasized the importance of a personal spiritual experience. Jesus said, "*The Kingdom of Heaven is within you*", The Buddha said "*Peace comes from within you, do not seek it without*", An Islamic proverb says, "*If you cannot find a temple in your heart, you will not find your heart in a temple*", and Krishna, in the Bhagavad Gita says to "*abandon all varieties of religion*". The Charge of The Goddess in modern paganism also states, "*If that which you seek cannot be found within, it will never be found without*". There is also a Hindu saying, "*What one does not trouble to find within will not be discovered by transporting the body hither and yon*".

True spirituality is not about making an outward show of worship or devotion to some external divine being. It is not about ritual or the performing of tasks and practices, it is about **realising** the connectedness to all that is, and to the creative energy that is as much you as is your skin.

I don't believe in an anthropomorphic god, a personal being that is somewhere out there, sitting on his throne in heaven. My understanding is that god is simply a name we have given to the fundamental creative energy that causes all things to be. Call it what you want, god, source, spirit, universe, whatever name you know it by, this energy is basic and flows through everything that is, and makes up everything that is. Therefore, the energy that is god is flowing through us and actually is us. There is no separating us from that which we call god.

One of the biggest lies that has been propagated by religion is that we are separated from god, that which is the creator of all things. This lie has been preached from pulpits and street corners throughout the centuries, and has been the biggest cause of denying us the reality of knowing our oneness with god, and with each other. In fact, this is something that I myself used to believe, having been taught it from childhood. There was a time in my life when this belief was so strong that I too used to try to convince others of what I thought was the truth. It could be said that I eventually "*saw the light*" and realised how misguided I had been to hold on to such a belief.

The church's story that we need a saviour to re-unite us with god, otherwise we are destined to spend eternity in hell, is in my opinion, absolutely ludicrous. If we look at the god of the Judaic Old Testament who is said to be all knowing and created everything that is, including the angel Lucifer, otherwise known as the devil or Satan, he knew when he created him that this Lucifer would "*fall from grace*". He would have known that this would result in sin coming into the world and people heading onwards on their journey to hell, where they would face eternal damnation. So, if god knew all this from the beginning, yet still went ahead with his plan he would be guilty of the most horrendous crimes ever committed. This image of god is a myth based entirely on fear.

I am blessed to have two beautiful daughters who, like all other children, have not always done as they were told. Imagine if I had punished them by locking them in a cellar and tormenting them for the rest of their lives just because they had not fitted in with the way I wanted them to live. Yet, this is the god that religion has told us about and has caused millions to fear. This is a god that is guilty of child-abuse, torture, mass-murder and just about every "*evil*" that you could think of. The world rightly recoiled in horror when the news came in 1998 of the case of Josef Fritzl. Fritzl kept his daughter imprisoned in a cellar for 24 years, yet many of those same people who reacted in such a way find it totally acceptable to worship a god, whom they believe sees it as right and just to condemn his children to an eternity in hell if they do not follow his ways. If it weren't for the fact that so many lives have been damaged, and much waste caused, by such teaching, it would be laughable. This man-made god does not exist and is most certainly not the image I want you to have when I use the word to describe the creative energy of the universe.

I want to emphasize again here that **it is not possible for us to be separated from god** because we are part of god, and god is part of us. Each one of us is in fact "god". Just as one can dip a glass into the ocean and examine the water therein, and discover that the water in the glass has exactly the same properties as the water still in the ocean, so we have all the same properties of the source from which we came.

Modern science, in the form of quantum physics, tells us that everything and everyone is connected, interdependent and one. Metaphysics teaches us of oneness, that all is one. It's not always easy to get your head round this one, especially when we see such a difference in people; good/bad, generous/greedy, selfish/benevolent, violent/ peaceful. How can I be one with Adolf Hitler or Pol Pot? To understand this takes a lot of shifting of old ideas, and taking on board some seemingly strange ones, but it is something that, if as I believe it to be right, has a massive effect on how one lives and relates to others. It encourages a greater awareness of the human race, our responsibilities and our actions.

Alongside the idea that we are all one, must run the idea that there is only one god. It has been said that "*all the gods are one god and all the goddesses are one goddess*". We call god by different names in order that we can relate to the concept and the reality of god. To some god is male, to others female, to even others, god is both male and female. Whether we call god Jehovah, Allah, Pan, Isis, Herne, Hecate, Source, Spirit, Universe, the Divine Energy, the Tao or George, it doesn't really matter, we use the name that helps us relate and understand. It doesn't alter the fact that there is only one creative energy whatever we perceive it to be.

When I was born, my parents, Violet and Trevor Reeves, named me John. My birth certificate bears the name John Reeves. I was often called Jim at school because of the popular country singer Jim Reeves, and eventually all my friends came to know me as Jim - Jim Reeves. When I embarked on a career as a professional musician I obviously couldn't use the name Jim Reeves and so I changed my name to Fox, Jim Fox. To some people I am still John Reeves, to others from a certain period of my life I am Jim Reeves and to most people today I am Jim Fox. It doesn't really matter what name I am known by, I am who I am, the three names belong to one person.

At different times of my life I have been known as different things to different people, including father, husband, writer, musician, sound-therapist, spiritual leader, but these are all simply labels. No matter how many different perceptions people have of me I am still me and there is only one me, constantly growing and expanding just like the universe that I am one with.

One god, one creation, one whole - **all is one and one is all**.

When we **realise** this and begin to experience it as a reality, we are on the way to living a fulfilled life, and a life of abundance, where we know that everything that we want and need, we already have, because we are at one with all things. It is then that we are on the way to extending the spiritual leg of the tripod to its perfect length.

I said at the outset that it is not my intention to tell you what you should do; you already have all the answers inside yourself, in that place of **Stillness**, deep within. I just want you to ask yourself, and in so doing discover your own answers.

So, what sort of questions am I suggesting that you

ask yourself?

How much thought and time do I give to my spiritual self on a normal day?

How often during the day do I take time to stop everything and ***Be Still****?*

Do I put in as much energy into my spiritual life as I do to watching the television or reading the news or engaging with social network sites on the internet?

When I listen to music am I filling my head with positive, uplifting sounds and words?

Do the books I read fill me with inspiration?

The words that I speak, do they bring blessing to those who hear me?

Is meditation something that I do only if I have the time and when everything else is done?

How do I start and finish each day?

Be Still and consider these questions and if you find that your answers are not in accordance with helping you to reach your full spiritual potential, resolve to change your habits and actions.

6

FINDING THE BALANCE - THE MENTAL AND EMOTIONAL

To date, no scientist has been able to actually pinpoint where the mind exists. Is it in the brain? Is it in the heart? Is it actually outside the body altogether? Scientists have debated this question for generations and so far they have been unable to discover its location or even how it really functions. One theory is that the mind is not actually limited to any one place in or around the human body, and this would seem to fit in with reports of out of body and near death experiences, where an individual's consciousness has been able to observe the body from outside the confines of the flesh and blood.

Wherever the mind is and however it works, one thing is for sure; our minds are full of millions of thoughts and ideas that come and go without invite and often without order. How many times have you sat down to relax, or to meditate, only to find the strangest thoughts coming into your mind? Thoughts about things you have done, things you are going to do, things you would like to do and of things that you have no idea why you are thinking them or where those thoughts came from. Negative thoughts, destructive thoughts, happy thoughts, sad thoughts, weird thoughts. We have millions of thoughts passing through our minds each day and these thoughts are often repeated from day to day.

To have a balanced and healthy mind we need to be aware of our thoughts and to exercise some sort of control over which thoughts we welcome and entertain. The thoughts that we allow to reside in our minds can have powerful effects over time. When we dwell on negative thinking, the thoughts behave like a cancer, continually growing and eating away at any positive thoughts until our mind becomes full of the negativity. Thoughts of criticism, thoughts of hate, thoughts of revenge, thoughts of greed, each thought taking up more time and space and crowding out the positive. If we can take control of our thoughts, and make a positive decision to entertain only good thoughts then we are on the path to finding balance in our mental lives.

I must confess that I do actually enjoy being part of the social media site, Facebook. I find it an excellent and accessible way to keep in touch with people and to connect with them. I also find it to be a valuable tool in promotion and marketing and as a means of spreading the message of Stillness. To me it is a means of being able to speak words of positivity to a large number of people in a place where I often see so much negativity. If you use Facebook yourself, (please feel free to visit my **Be Still** page and link up to it), you will have no doubt seen the numerous status updates where people seem to complain and whine about everything from the weather to another's political views, from the latest celebrity news to the state of the economy. It is my belief that dwelling on negativity breeds even more negativity, and the more we dwell on these harmful thought vibrations, the more we are likely to express similar thoughts.

If you use social network sites why not make a determined resolution to post only updates and comments that are positive and uplifting, praising people and complimenting them, sharing their happiness and your own positivity. For those of you who are not part of such social networking sites, you can do the same with your everyday conversations at work, at the bus stop, on the train, in the café or at home. As negativity breeds negativity, so positivity breeds positivity.

The apostle Paul writes in the sacred book of the Christian path:

"Whatsoever things are ***true****, whatsoever things are* ***honest****, whatsoever things are* ***just****, whatsoever things are* ***pure****, whatsoever things are* ***lovely****, whatsoever things are* ***of good report****; if there be any* ***virtue****, and if there be any* ***praise****, think on these things."*

By making a conscious decision to only allow thoughts that are productive and wholesome to take root in our minds, we are not allowing the negative and destructive thoughts room to develop and grow. That's not to say that these "*bad*" thoughts are not going to surface, but when they do, you just take hold of them and say, "*there is no space in my mind to dwell on you, please go away and don't come back - you are not welcome here*".

First thing when you wake up in the morning, start this discipline and bring to mind all the things that are **true** in your life. Start with the basic truths. *"I am alive, my heart is beating, I am breathing",* it could be true that you have a roof over your head, a comfortable bed to sleep in, food on the table, a loving family. Thoughts are a form of energy and continually thinking about the same thing serves to add energy and strength to that thing you are thinking about. If you are continually worrying about something such as, "*I'm not going to have enough money to pay the bills next month*" or "*I'm frightened that I might develop cancer or some other terrible illness*" you are only feeding those fears. Those worries and fears are not "true" thoughts, you cannot know that it is true that you won't have the money or that you might get ill. You cannot know that if you have been diagnosed with an illness that you won't recover. At many times in my life I have worried about financial problems and the more I have worried, the bigger those problems seem to become. However, I learnt that worrying only adds fuel to the fire. I began to **realise** that, whilst I still might not have the money today for a bill that is coming in next month, anything can happen between now and then. I'm just going to be grateful for what I have got now and think about that instead, and in so doing I am adding energy to the truth that I have sufficient for the moment. By doing so, I find that the state of sufficiency continues, and when the time arrives to pay the bill arrives, the means to pay it also manifests itself.

Whatever things are true for you, think about them, and the more you think about them the more the feeling of gratitude will rise up within you and you will begin to **realise** abundance in your life.

Think about things that are **honest**, things that are genuine, upright and fair. In your relationships and dealings with others there may be times when you are tempted to be somewhat less than honest. When that happens, immediately take hold of those thoughts before allowing them to take root and once again say to them, *"there is no place in my mind for such thoughts, please go away and don't return"*. Train your mind to think honestly and you will find that in your life you become honorable in your principles, intentions, and actions. The one who thinks honest thoughts is an honest person.

Let your thoughts be **just**. It is so easy to be judgmental towards situations and people. We hear something and are often quick to make a judgment without knowing the complete facts. The next time you find yourself in that situation, hold back and refrain from making a judgment that may just turn out to be wrong. Exercise justice in your thinking. Judgmental and condemnatory thoughts have a habit of turning round and bringing judgment and condemnation on the thinker.

I don't believe that judgment itself is wrong; I don't actually believe that it is possible to go through life without judging. Every day we make judgments. We judge whether it is safe to cross the road without getting run over. We judge whether something is too hot to handle. We judge whether the offer we have just been made really is too good to be true. We judge whether it is safe to trust a particular individual. Paraphrasing the words that the teacher Jesus is reported to have said: "*you will be judged in the manner in which you judge*". Basically this means that if you act with justice towards others, others will treat you with justice. I don't believe that he is saying that we should never make judgments, but rather that when you judge, be mindful of judging with fairness and in a just manner.

Only allow your mind to entertain **pure** thoughts. Don't harbour thoughts that are contaminated and infected with what is not good and wholesome. Sometimes we may find ourselves thinking thoughts that might be stained in some way, dishonest thoughts, hurtful thoughts, distorted or twisted thoughts, inflammatory thoughts or thoughts that are just plain wrong. Once again when such thoughts enter your mind, don't panic, don't feel guilty, just acknowledge them and say, "*I only have room for pure, wholesome thoughts that if spoken aloud would only bring blessing and benefit to those who would hear them*". It is so important to be mindful of our thoughts and to exercise a measure of discipline so that we are aware of which thoughts we are allowing to take up residence in our minds, and to be ready to evict any thoughts that do not bring joy and peace into our lives.

Allow your thoughts to dwell on that which is **lovely** rather than that which is ugly. Think of the good things in life, the beautiful things around you in nature, the beautiful people and places in your life, the things that make you feel good. When we read the newspapers or watch the news on television or listen to it on the radio, it is easy to get caught up in seeing all the bad things that are happening, that is how newspapers sell and how news programmes get their viewers and listeners. Just remember that there is so much more that is good in the world than there is that is bad. For every murderer there are millions of loving, caring people. For every plane crash, there are thousands of flights that take off and land safely, for every natural disaster that occurs there is day after day after day of normal everyday life, for every war zone there are a multitude of peaceful lands. Too easily we tend to look at the distressing things, especially if we have watched the TV news late at night before going to bed, we lie in bed thinking of what we have seen and heard when we could be thinking of all the wonderful, lovely things in our world. By thinking in this way before we go to sleep we not only positively influence our dreams but also prepare ourselves for waking up with positive thoughts in the morning, ready to start the day on the right footing.

I'm not suggesting here, as some people do, that we should not listen to the news or read the papers. Doing so gives us information on what is going on in the world and where we can best use our energies to make the world a better place. When we hear of natural disasters such as floods, tornadoes, earthquakes etc. we have knowledge of where we can help either in material ways by donating money or clothing or simply by offering up prayers/mantras/healing thoughts for the people and places affected. When a child goes missing we can again send our prayers and maybe even offer practical help by joining in the search. What I am suggesting is that we filter out the news that we hear and read in order to be able to give of our energies rather than dwelling on the doom and gloom.

When you hear criticism of another, pointing out their failings and shortcomings, their mistakes or even their intentional wrongdoings, don't dwell on it by continuing to think about what you have heard, read or seen. Thinking in such a way is not going to do you or the other person any good at all. By allowing such thoughts to linger you are opening yourself to so many things that may harm you and your relationships; mistrust, fear, jealousy, anger, hatred, all of these are things that will eat away at you.

Dismiss such thoughts and think of the good things you know and have heard. Whatever is of **good report**, think on that. We are all probably familiar with the words that the teacher, Jesus, said, "*Let him who is without sin cast the first stone*". There is not one of us who has not done or said something in our lives that has been out of order or caused hurt to another, whether intentionally or not. That does not make us a bad person. I don't personally believe that anyone is either totally bad or totally good, like a coin there are two sides to each of us. Admittedly sometimes one side shows up more than the other, a lot more in some cases, but that does not define the whole person. Remember that we are all part of and connected to that which we call god, it is just that some allow the nature of god to flow through, whereas others have blocked it off. This is an area where **forgiveness** comes in and it is something that we will look at more deeply later on. Remember, "*whatsoever things are **of good report**; if there be any **virtue**, and if there be any **praise**, think on these things*"

*

One of the questions I suggested at the end of the last section on spirituality, related to the type of music we might listen to. I have learned after many years of working in the music industry to be more discerning and selective about what I actually listen to. You know what it is like when the words of a song that you have heard, or remember from the past, get stuck on a loop in your head? This is all very well if the words are edifying but if those words are negative or destructive then that energy is feeding on your mind and taking up the time and space that could be occupied by positive thinking. I am sure that many of you reading this book will be familiar with the work of Masaru Emoto. The renowned Japanese scientist shows evidence that thoughts, words and music, have a direct effect on molecules of water. In his books he reproduces photographs of crystals formed in frozen water after thoughts and sounds have been directed at them. There is an amazing contrast in the crystals formed in water that has been exposed to positive, loving energy to that of water exposed to negative energy. The water that has received positive energy such as love, calming music, peaceful and encouraging words, produces beautiful crystals like snowflakes, whereas the water exposed to words and thoughts such as hate or violence, as well as loud heavy music with negative lyrics, results in dull, distorted crystals. Bearing in mind that we are made up of something like 75% water, it is so important to be mindful of what we are hearing and thinking and its effect on us.

Experiments carried out in greenhouses have shown that when loudspeakers are placed near to growing plants and light classical and Indian classical music is played, the plants started to lean towards the speakers. When loud, aggresive rock music was played the plants began to lean away from the speakers. Also the soft classical music caused the plants to flourish, whilst continued exposure to the aggressive music resulted in the plants becoming stunted with some failing to bloom entirely.

Be careful what you listen to. Fill your mind with that which is good and wholesome. When we **Abide in the Stillness** one of the things that is happening is that we are cleansing our mind, clearing out all the clutter and background noise that would pollute our being; releasing all the blockages that would stand in the way of allowing the flow of abundance in our lives.

7

FINDING THE BALANCE - THE MATERIAL

Throughout the years that I have been following what might be termed an holistic lifestyle, I have found that when it comes to the material world people often fall into one of two camps. The first is made up of those who believe that to be spiritual means turning your back on all things material, particularly when it comes to luxuries. They have a belief that it is a sign of spirituality to have little and to shy away from anything that goes beyond the basic necessities for living. I have come across many therapists and healers who seem to be embarrassed about charging a financial fee for the treatments and services which they offer, some even go as far as to think that it is wrong, as if having to exchange money for such things is something dirty and to be avoided.

At the other end of the scale is the thinking that to have much and to have it in abundance is a sign of true spirituality because god, or the universe, is blessing them with a bounty of gifts. Much of this thinking seems to come from the recent plethora of books on such things as the law of attraction and the secret to getting everything that you ask for.

I really feel that both these camps are missing the point and that the truth lies somewhere between the two. We don't need to be afraid of having money or material things, neither should we see the amassing of wealth as a goal or a priority. I have already mentioned that, for me, abundance is having enough so that I can share, it isn't about how much I can manifest for myself, it's not about storing up for a rainy day, it is not about greed, it is about being able to circulate what comes, so that those who have, are able to share and help those who have not. It has been said that if you want to create abundance for yourself, first create it for somebody else. What you wish for yourself, wish for others. Have a healthy respect for money and material blessings but don't see that as an end, view yourself as being a channel for money to flow in fairness and without favour. Remember that our purpose in this life is not to get, but to give.

The universe/god does not want us to suffer in anyway whatsoever. The universe is abundant and limitless and we are one with that source, therefore it is our natural state to be living in abundance and without limit. We can enjoy abundance in wealth and abundance in health; god does not need because god is everything. A particularly good affirmation to use is:

"I have no need of anything, I already have everything. I enjoy abundant wealth, abundant health, abundant life."

Whatever is necessary for our life we are able to manifest through our oneness with the divine creative energy. God is creator, I am creator. The problem comes when we see manifestation as being the goal, the pinnacle, when we say *"I am able to manifest whatever I want, therefore I am living a spiritual life".* Let me tell you now that just because you have understood and are able to utilize the law of attraction does not make you spiritual, neither is it a sign of enlightenment.

I recently heard somebody talking about their ability to manifest certain things, particularly cars. He was very proud that he was the owner of 5 top-of-the-range vehicles parked on his driveway. One has to ask, is this spirituality or greed? We are talking about balance here and balance is about allowing things to flow out as well as flowing in. We don't need to put a limit on how much flows in, neither do we put a limit on how much flows out. There is nothing wrong with manifesting 5 cars but you can only drive one at a time, I guess the thing to do with the other 4 would be to make them available to people who do not have cars of their own to drive, but if they are just standing on the driveway the only thing being created is stagnation.

Again, let me emphasize, the material world with all its bounty is not something to be shied away from or rejected. As a spiritual being you have chosen to be incarnated into a material presence in a material world with all that goes along with such an existence. You have a physical body with physical needs and desires. There is nothing wrong with acknowledging those needs and desires. Your body requires food and clothing, it requires shelter and it has every right to be comfortable. The problem comes when we are attached to the outcome of our needs and desires.

I can enjoy the pleasure of a good meal, a comfortable home, a reliable vehicle to transport me. I can enjoy the luxuries of life - a relaxing holiday, a night at the theatre or a concert, a day of being "spoilt" with the chance to put my feet up. The key is to not see these things as essential to my existence or necessary to my fulfilment and happiness. My priority is to be living in oneness with the universal divine presence not to be "*storing up treasures on earth*". In his teachings, Jesus made it clear that focusing on gathering to one's self is futile as everything will just fade away, be eaten by moths or rust, so all your efforts are, in the end, worthless. However, he also said that by "*seeking first the kingdom (realm) of god, all these things will be added to you*". It is a matter of intention and priority, and our motives need to be pure. It would be totally pointless, and indeed selfish and self-defeating, if we tried to live a spiritual life simply in order to receive reward, whether that reward is material in this life or the promise of blessing in a life to come.

Living in tune with the natural world.

When looking at the spiritual we considered the beliefs we allow into our lives, with the mental we talked about being mindful of the thoughts, words and music we allow in and now with the material, or physical aspect I would ask you to be also mindful of the foods we allow into our bodies and to make a decision to take in a balanced, nutritious and wholesome diet rather than filling ourselves with processed, chemically altered, genetically modified, unhealthy food.

It has been said that everything that we do is either based on fear or love. The subject of food is one of those areas that is often rife with fear-based stories about what to eat and what not to eat, which foods are harmful and likely to cause illness. So before you read the next couple of paragraphs I want to, once again, draw your attention to some words of Jesus when he said, "*It is not what goes into the mouth that defiles the man, but rather that which comes out of his mouth (or heart)*".

The work of Dr Masaru Emoto and his experiments with the power of thought and intention on water shows how positive and loving energy has an effect on the water. It is my belief that by showing our appreciation for our food and "blessing" it with our thoughts or prayers can actually ensure that what we are eating is good for us and will provide us with all the nutrition that we need. Having said that, it is still important that we are responsible and mindful when it comes to what we eat.

Nature is a wonderful thing; it provides us with all that we need, when we need it. It is not by accident that certain foods grow at specific times of the year, it is for our benefit and well-being. These days we can go into a supermarket and buy foods that have been produced out of season or imported from countries in the opposite hemisphere to where we live. Even if we put aside the very important environmental issues of eating out of season, the cost of transport, forced growing, chemical use etc., we can still see that for our own good we ought to be living in tune with nature, which of course is part of the manifestation of the divine creative source.

The natural cycle of crops is the way it is for a perfectly good reason. Winter foods are usually of the warming varieties that heat you up during the cold months. In the summer time, nature provides us with cooling foods to help keep your temperature level in the warmer weather. By eating out of season we are not receiving any of the benefits that nature intends for us and we are more than likely doing ourselves more harm than good. Fruit and vegetables produced out of season have reduced nutritional value. By introducing preservatives to our food we are losing nutrients and the health benefits of such foods are diminished. Natural seasonal foods contain antioxidants that not only help to keep you young but also help to repel illness and disease by nurturing the immune system. By eating seasonal foods we are in balance with the rhythms of nature intended to keep us in good health.

*

Okay, so let's go back to the camera on the tripod. By following the suggestions and teachings you have just read, you will be able to adjust the balance of the legs of the tripod - the spiritual, mental and material, and through the viewfinder of the camera you will start to see a more balanced picture of the world, seeing life as it really is - a balance of the material, the emotional and the spiritual.

When we change the way we see life and view it with a sense of balance we also start to change the way we think about what is important in our lives, what we want and what we need. We put a different value on all aspects of life and acknowledge that just enjoying material abundance does not bring satisfaction. We also see that having knowledge on its own does not bring about fulfillment and neither does being spiritually aware necessarily mean that our life is complete.

An abundant life is a balanced life.

A balanced life is an abundant life.

8

FEAR OR LOVE?

It has been said that everything that we do is either motivated by fear or by love. These two powerful energies are the driving forces for our actions, our words and our thoughts. The choice that we make as to whether we decide to live a life based on fear or on love has a direct effect on whether we are to enjoy a life of abundance, or a life of lack.

I know from personal experience that I have missed out on something in life that probably would have brought me a lot of pleasure and enjoyment, I also know that nobody is to blame for this and I take complete responsibility for not fulfilling my potential in this particular area. I never succeeded in learning to swim. As a child I used to watch my friends in the swimming pool splashing about, having fun, diving into the water and obviously enjoying the experience of swimming, while not only would I stay in the shallow end, but I wouldn't actually be able to let go of the rail at the edge of the pool. The fear of not being able to float, and the thought of swallowing the water, together with coughing and gasping for air, held me back.

Exactly the same thing happened on the one occasion that I visited an ice-skating rink. While everybody else was gliding around on the ice, I stayed at the edge holding on to the bar, frightened of falling and making a fool of myself.

I was convinced that if I let go, I would fall. I also knew that the only way I could possibly achieve the success of swimming or skating was, in fact, to let go of that which I felt was keeping me safe. The problem was that I did feel safe by holding on. I was safe, but I was missing out.

So often we miss out on the fullness of life and living in abundance because we hold on to what we believe to be safe, even though we know that we are not satisfied or living in accordance with our full potential. We feel restricted and frustrated in our work, our careers, when what we really want to do is something that we know would give us more pleasure and fulfillment - but at least we know that it is safe. We feel limited and perhaps trapped by being in a relationship that we know is keeping us from being who we truly are, but that relationship has been there for some time and we are afraid to let go, holding on to that misguided sense of security. "*Better the devil you know*" could be said to be the mantra of one who misses out on the opportunities and abundant fullness of life.

If what you are doing is not bringing you joy and fulfillment in your life, step back, **Abide in the Stillness,** and ask what it is that would bring you joy. Be willing to let go of that which appears to be safe yet in reality is unfulfilling, and experience the buoyancy of being upheld by the water.

If you have always wanted to play music - start playing music.

If you have always wanted to paint pictures - go out and buy the brushes and start painting.

If you've always wanted to write - start writing.

If you've always wanted to care and nurse people, take the steps to make it happen.

If the job you are doing or the relationship you are in is

holding you back from being fulfilled - make the move, make it happen.

Whatever it is that you believe you should be doing in your life, you have the freedom to do it. The only thing that is really holding you back is the fear to let go of what you are clinging on to and to reach out for that which you love.

"But I've got a mortgage to pay, a family to provide for. How can I just let go and do the things I want to do?"

The simple key is to **Be Still** and then to **Live in that Stillness**, and know that your desires or goals are in alignment with the universal energy; with god. If your inner voice, your spirit, affirms a congruency with the greater purpose of the universe, I believe you can feel secure in the knowledge that all things are working together for good. Let me remind you again of the words I quoted earlier: *"Seek first the kingdom (realm, place) of god (universe, source) and all these things shall be added unto you"*. In other words, focus on the source of all things; align yourself with the divine mind, which we call god, and everything that you need to "be" is yours for the asking.

Another hindrance to **realising** abundance in our lives is the belief that we "need" things, and the fear that we may lose what we already have. We are all familiar with the phrase "*less is more*", which is used in a variety of contexts today including decoration, ornamentation etc. The truth is that "*less is more*" is a great lesson to learn when it come to knowing abundance in our lives.

In modern society there is a great emphasis on growth and accumulation. We hear our politicians talking about the importance of economic growth all the time. We live in a world where it is considered normal and natural to want more of everything, more money, a bigger house, a job with more responsibility, more possessions etc. I want to suggest something to you that might sound strange or even seem to be a contradiction. I want to suggest that having less can be a key to enjoying and experiencing abundance.

When we **realise** that we don't actually need all the stuff we accumulate in our lives, when we **realise** that we don't actually need a fortune to provide all that we really do need to live, when we **realise** that happiness and fulfillment is not about what we have stored away for a rainy day, we then begin to **realise** that we are already living a life of abundance.

It is amazing how much "stuff" we accumulate over the years without even recognizing that we are doing so. My wife and I recently moved home from a reasonably sized three-bedroomed house into a modest one-bedroom, one reception room cottage. We decided that we did not need such a large place; after all you can only be in one room at a time. We had no need for three bedrooms when it was only the two of us who live in the house and we rarely had overnight guests staying with us. In our new compact cottage we are still able to accommodate visitors from time to time by making use of the sofa bed in the lounge.

However, moving to a much smaller home meant that an awful lot of "stuff" had to go, as there was no room for it anymore. With the help of eBay, car-boot sales and drop-offs at charity shops we were able to re-allocate furniture, white goods, an oven, books, CDs, ornaments, clothes and tools in such a way that people who needed them more than we did, were able to take possession of them at minimum expense. Downsizing and shedding all this surplus stuff was an amazingly liberating and cathartic experience that has enabled us to appreciate the abundance that we have in our lives. When the decision was made to take this course of action there was no fear that having fewer possessions would make us lesser individuals, rather there was an awareness of the sense of love that we could share as we passed on what we no longer had need of for ourselves.

Feeling secure as you **Abide in the Stillness** and have the knowledge that you are not what you have, can be an amazingly liberating experience as you become willing and able to free yourself from the bondage of too many possessions.

9

MANY PARTS - ONE WHOLE

Science and spirituality are often viewed as being at opposite ends of the spectrum, so I find it both exciting and encouraging that these two areas are now merging in so many ways. When Albert Einstein presented his general theory of relativity and theorised that there is a space-time connection and that matter is inseparable from an omnipresent quantum energy field, science was coming into alignment with what spiritual teachers and traditions had been speaking about for thousands of years. Everything is connected, everyone is connected. Together, all things make up the one whole.

Yet, this does not mean that because we are all one we are not individuals, and do not have our own individual personalities and qualities. Just like the bones in your body are all different, yet together make up the one "you", so we are all different but make up the "one".

A physical body is made up of many different parts: bones, organs, skin, hair etc. Each individual part is different and unique. If we take a look at the adult human skeleton, we will discover that it is made up of 206 bones, each one different but each one playing its own individual part in the whole. It is no use the tibia wanting to be a scapula. The incus in the middle ear could not fulfill the role of the patella, neither could the tibia take the place of the occipital bone. Each bone has its own place, in the same way that we each have our own role to play in the greater body of the divine universe.

Each of us has a purpose in life, our dharma, and it is a role that only we can fulfill. The spiritual teachings of the New Testament speak of the believers being the *"Body of Christ".* I'd like you, if you can, to put aside the old paradigm of thinking of *Christ* as a person. I don't believe that that is what is meant in this phrase or description of the "*Body of Christ*". If we think of it instead as "the Christ body", the Christ-energy or Christ-consciousness, which is not limited to one physical existence, but is the creative source of life itself, then we can see how this analogy of the body actually works.

To deny one's individuality is to shirk from the responsibility of being that which one really is. If we deny our purpose as an individual and don't fulfill our dharma then the whole is being deprived of something important and is unable to function to its fullness.

We become aware of our individual place in the body when we find and connect with the stillness inside, the divine spark of life which is part of the creative energy of all things and which is our soul. It is so important to know who we are and what is our dharma, our purpose, our role. As we live and dwell in the stillness, so we become aware, and as we acknowledge that "calling" we can then fulfill what it is that we are here for. Nothing is an accident. You are not an accident, you are here for a reason and no one else can fulfill that role. In the same way, you cannot fulfill the role of another. It is no good you looking at others and wanting to be them, to be someone or something that you are not. The foot doesn't say, *"I want to be an elbow"*, the big toe doesn't say *"I could be a better knee-cap than the one that is already there".*

Your dharma is to be who you are and to fulfill your purpose in life. That purpose might be to be a writer or a janitor, it might be to be a teacher or carer. Nothing and no one is more important or more valuable than another.

You are important as you are. If you are not fulfilling your dharma then the whole is not functioning as it should. If the knee were not there, then the leg would not bend.

When I am in the right place then I am playing my part in completing the big picture. I am then not only adding to the universal abundance, I am also in a position to enjoy that abundance. If I am not in the right place, then something is missing from the whole and not only is it me who is missing out on that experience of fullness, I am also depriving others of enjoying that experience.

Take time to **Be Still** and to know your right place in the whole, and on knowing your right place, be willing to take up residence there like a piece of a jig-saw puzzle completing the picture.

10

WALKING THE LABYRINTH

Once you have spent time in the stillness and you have caught sight of the direction your life is heading in, your purpose or dharma, then comes the question,

"How do I get from where I am now, to the place in which I am fulfilling my dharma?"

There was a time, some years ago, when I knew in my heart what I should be doing with my life. The trouble was that I had no idea how I could get from the position that I was in then, to that place that I believed was where I should be, and doing what it was that I believed I should be doing. It seemed to be an impossible dream. Whichever way I looked at it, I couldn't see how I could do it. All I could see were the obstacles, the lack of financial resources, and the other commitments that were taking up my time. How could I possibly get from here to there? Then, one day the answer came to me so clearly and so simply; an answer that had been there all along.

My wife, Kiera, and I had organised a Healing Camp in West Wales, where we had gathered together a number of healers and practitioners who were offering their services and leading workshops throughout the weekend. The centrepiece of the camp was a beautiful Cretan labyrinth, which had been made by some friends. After the opening ceremony, the labyrinth was open for people to use as a meditation throughout the weekend. One of the purposes of a labyrinth meditation is that if you have a specific question or dilemma that you are looking for an answer to, you enter the labyrinth with that as your focus and by the time you either reach the centre, or leave the labyrinth, you are ready to receive the wisdom.

Kiera and I entered the labyrinth together, knowing that we both shared a vision without knowing how to accomplish, or manifest that vision. I didn't have to wait until we reached the centre of the labyrinth before receiving my answer. As soon as I made my first step onto the path, I knew. It was clear and simple, just like a light being switched on in my soul. People often confuse a labyrinth with a maze, when they are in fact two totally different things. When you walk through a maze you are confronted with turnings, which may lead you to a dead-end, causing frustration and a lot of wasted time. When you walk a labyrinth however, there is only one path. At times it may seem that the path is taking you round in circles and further away from your destination, but that one path will always lead you to the centre. I knew then that in order to reach the place that was my goal, my purpose, all I had to do was to keep walking. As I took one step at a time, followed the path and kept moving, I was heading towards my destination. Yes, there would be times when it would feel like I was moving further away, or going round in circles without making any progress, but I knew that if I just kept going and moving forwards then I could not fail to reach the centre, my destination, my purpose, my dharma.

What a simple revelation this was for me. What a fantastic lesson to learn.

Once you have spent time in the **Stillness** and you have caught sight of the direction your life is heading in; your purpose or dharma, all you need to do is to keep moving and following your path, and by so doing you cannot fail to reach your goal. Simply keep your focus and intention on that which is your vision, **walk with Stillness in your soul** and that divine energy, whatever name you wish to give it, will ensure that you will not fail. Even when you might feel that it is too hard or that there are just too many obstacles, or even that you are just getting nowhere, the only thing you have to do is to follow the path as it unfolds before you and, with the universe providing all that you need from a boundless storehouse of abundance, you will reach your destination.

11

BACK TO THE GARDEN

Over the last couple of years, Kiera and I have made two house moves. 18 months before our latest move into the cottage in which we now live, we moved to a house in a small village in West Wales. Apart from the fact that it was in such a peaceful setting in a beautiful area of the country, one of the things that drew us to it was the wonderful garden. I'll try to describe it for you if I may. As you exited the house from the back door, a pathway divided the garden as it led to the fields behind the house. On the right hand side of the path was a herb-garden where a variety of culinary and aromatic herbs gave a wonderful scent, particularly in the early evening. Beyond the herbs was a row of buildings - a workshop, toolshed and wood store. Then came the vegetable garden and finally a poly-tunnel, which housed the tomato plants and various other vegetables. To the left of the path was the rose-garden and then the pond, which had all sorts of life, including tadpoles, dragon-flies, newts etc. After this, and separated by some shrubbery we had a lovely grassy area with seats and space to enjoy the wonderful Welsh sunshine that we enjoyed during our time there, and finally we had half-a-dozen fruit trees and a few fruit bushes along the wall before the compost stores.

I used to love to walk in the garden and watch the birds feeding as I would check on the growth of the many different flowers, shrubs and trees, appreciating the wonders of nature as the plants managed to keep going whether they were subjected to the freezing cold of winter or the heat of summer. I also enjoyed the process of planting seeds and tending them as they grew, before planting them out in the garden. There is so much that we can learn from the garden that can be used in our development of a life of abundance.

When we have been to that place of **Stillness** deep within, and we have a vision of something that we should aspire to or something that we need to aid us on our journey to **realising** our purpose, we can liken this to preparing the soil in readiness for the next stage.

The next stage, of course, is to plant the seed. We take the seed of our vision, or our desire if you like, and place it just below the surface of the earth. And then we leave it. We don't keep returning to it, removing the top layer of soil to see how it is progressing. We leave it buried and allow it to germinate and eventually sprout into new growth. We trust that nature will work its magic and we let it get on with its job.

Do you hear what I am saying here? Once you have made your connection with the divine source and you have a clear vision of where you should be going, or who you should be, when you see what it is that you need to manifest that vision, you then need to allow that seed to be planted in your soul, covering it and protecting it with your trust and belief that the universe is working for good. You don't need to keep digging it up, checking it and replanting it, just let it rest and give it chance to grow.

Now that isn't to say that you just sit back and do nothing, like any good gardener there is still work to be done in looking after your seed. The soil needs to be watered and nourished, and any weeds that appear need to be pulled out and removed.

Let's look at how we water and feed the seed as it begins to grow. It is important to keep that connection between the spirit that is you and the greater spirit that is the divine source of all that is. In that union, in that connection you become one with the life-giving energy that will continue to feed and nourish the seed that you have planted in your soul. As you abide in the Stillness, so you will know yourself as a channel for the "living waters" which will bring growth and fruition to that which you have planted. **Be Still**, don't fret about how it is going to grow. Don't worry about whether its shoots can break through the darkness of the earth; just allow it to be what it is.

It is pretty much inevitable that other things are going to start to grow in your soul apart from that seed which you want to see flourishing. These weeds will maybe start off as negative thoughts or doubts that come into your mind. Don't worry about that, just see them for what they are - they are just thoughts which you can acknowledge, then take hold of, pluck them out and cast them away. When these thoughts or doubts come in, say to them "*I* ***recognise*** *you for what you are and right now there is no place for you in my being, so I am not giving you the space or the opportunity to grow and take over from what is my purpose.*"

Another type of weed that you may encounter is "time". You may feel that all the mundane things that you think you have to do are crowding you out and so restricting the growth of your seedling. Again, you are in control here. If too many things are happening in your life and taking up too much time, do some weeding. Clear out the things that are growing and taking over so that you can allow space and time for the seed of your purpose to flourish and become strong.

I think it is worth me repeating something I just said in the last paragraph - "***You are in control***".

You are not a puppet. There is no anthropomorphic god dictating everything that happens in your life. There is no predestined plan for your life. We, each one of us, have a responsibility to take responsibility for our own lives.

So, if the seed that you have planted is to grow, then you have to help it to grow by looking after it and getting rid of anything that might hinder its growth. You also have to allow it to grow in its own time, without forcing it or interfering with it. If you follow these two principles then you are guaranteed to witness that which is in harmony with your divine purpose, or dharma, come to abundant fruition.

When it came to harvesting we were blessed with an abundance of tomatoes, sweet potatoes, leeks, swede, lettuce, squash, sweetcorn, peas, beans, beetroot, carrots, parsnips, sprouts, and onions along with apples, grapes, blackberries, raspberries, strawberries, logan berries. "*Abundant*" really is the only word to describe that harvest.

12

ALL IN GOOD TIME

Once we have a clear vision of our dharma and we start out on our journey towards that goal, it is amazing how things start to happen. Things that some might call co-incidences but which I prefer to call divine synchronicity. Often referred to by Swiss psychologist, Carl Gustav Jung, synchronicity is when a number of events or situations come together in a seemingly random way, but actually have meaning and purpose without causality. Sometimes you just seem to be in the right place at the right time, and what may appear to be a chance encounter has an important influence on your life and direction. I've experienced this many times throughout my life and, while I used to consider it to be amazing, I now understand that this is just the way it is.

My mother and father were both diagnosed with terminal cancer within two weeks of each other, and they died just four months apart. During the period of their illness I spent much of my time living with them, caring for them and offering support. It was an incredible time of learning for me and was to have a profound effect on my life. I actually count it a blessing and a privilege to have been able to spend time with them both during their last days, and to have been with them at the moment they moved on from this physical life. My wife, Kiera, is both a palliative care nurse and a Soul Midwife. In both these roles she is caring for, and offering support to those who are dying. We both received a very clear vision that part of our purpose together was to build on our experiences, to set up a centre where we could offer holistic and complementary therapies, to those living with life-limiting illnesses and also for their carers.

This is the vision we were both holding when we entered the labyrinth that I spoke about earlier. We knew that this was part of our purpose, our dharma together. There was no doubt about it but, as I mentioned before, we had no idea how we could bring it about.

At the time, I was renting a room above an holistic shop where I was practicing Sound Therapy. Unfortunately the shop wasn't doing too well and the owner took the decision to close the business, which meant I was going to be without a therapy room. The date for closure was set as 28th February 2011. Two weeks before the shop was due to close, I received a phone call saying that I had been chosen to appear on a television game show, and I would need to be available for 3 weeks beginning March 1st, in order to start recording. The timing was perfect, it was to be the day after the shop was closing, and it looked like things were beginning to move forwards. This was an opportunity to get some money to enable us to start taking steps towards our dream. Another aspect of this perfect timing, was that I was required to be at the TV studios for one week, before a break of a week and then returning to complete the recording the following week. Perfect, because I was committed to exhibit and speak at a Mind, Body, and Spirit event during that week between recordings. This meant that I was able to go on the show and still be available to honour my previous commitment.

The show was "*Deal or No Deal*" and was hosted by Noel Edmonds, a popular TV presenter here in Britain, and a former DJ. Noel is also very interested in the principles of the law of attraction and cosmic ordering and he has himself written a book on the subject called "Positively Happy – Cosmic Ways to Change Your Life" published by Random House. When the time came to play my game, Kiera and I were able to talk on air about our vision of the holistic centre and working with cancer patients and others who had life-limiting conditions. Our words were to be broadcast to around 2 million people across the UK. We walked away from the show with a cheque for £15,000, which was the start of something that was to continue to grow over the coming months.

When the show was aired in the following November, one particular viewer was reminded of a similar vision that she had had many years before, but for one reason or another she had never seen it come to fruition. She felt that she wanted to help but at the time had no spare money to offer. We received a letter from her the following March in which she told us that on March 1st, exactly one year after I walked into the television studio, she had won a substantial sum on the monthly Premium Bond draw and subsequently sent us a cheque for £20,000. During that year, and following my "*light-bulb moment*" in the labyrinth we received over £65,000 from various, and unexpected, sources.

*

After looking at a number of likely premises over the next few months, it once again seemed like we weren't getting anywhere. The places were either too big or too small, or in need of too much work. One place that we were really interested in and for which we were in the process of making an offer, fell through at the last minute which was disappointing at the time, but with hind-sight it was a good thing, as developments that took place in the area during the following months would have made things such as car-parking and access very difficult. We knew we were following the right path, so made the decision to stop trying to force it, as this was only causing us to get stressed with the frustration of hitting brick walls, and instead just wait until the right place revealed itself to us.

It was not too long afterwards that I was paying a visit to the bank, I had parked in a car-park that I had used before on many occasions, and I happened to notice a sign in a building opposite saying "*office space to rent*". Thinking that this might give us somewhere to offer our therapies from whilst we continued to look for something more permanent, I called in to make enquiries. It immediately felt right and after talking to the present occupier and explaining our vision to him, what was initially two or three rooms being available, turned into the whole building, as he then decided that he would re-locate his whole business so that we could take over the entire premises. I had simply been in the right place at the right time.

Within four weeks we had moved in to what is now known as The Centre. Another amazing thing about this was that a few doors away an entirely different business was opening up, and it had taken them 9 months from the time of making an offer to actually moving in, and they were dealing with the same agent that we were! The universe was certainly working for us and with us.

We now have The Centre up and running at the premises, which contains a number of therapy rooms as well as the reception area, a workshop space for classes and groups and a meditation space. In the following couple of months we set to work on what was a very overgrown garden area and turned it into our Peace Garden, complete with summer-house, which can also be used as a therapy and meditation space. At the time of writing we have 12 therapists working from The Centre providing a wide range of treatments and consultations and we are also able to offer services to those with life-limiting illnesses, and their carers, on either a free or a donation basis.

The lesson here is that when you have made connection with the **Stillness within,** and you have a vision of your purpose, then the universe has a way of bringing things together and providing all that is needed to make things happen.

All we have to do is keep walking in the right direction and to surrender to the now.

13

MIND THE GAP

It has often been said that when we listen to a piece of music, it is the gap between the notes that make the sounds enjoyable. If it were not for the gaps, then all the notes would join together and we would be left with just a noise. When we listen to someone speaking, again it is the gap between the words that make the sentence comprehensible. If it were not for the gaps, and all the words were rolled into one, it would be impossible to fully understand the meaning of the words and the sentiment behind the words.

To be in the Stillness is to be in the gap. The gap between all the thoughts in your mind. The gap between all the activities in your life. The place that offers understanding and meaning to our lives on this planet. The place that makes sense of it all.

On the London Underground system, when the train was coming to a stop at the station, passengers would hear a recorded voice with the message “mind the gap”, as a reminder to be aware of the gap between the carriage and the platform. The recorded message was withdrawn from use a few years ago, but I recently read that the widow of the actor whose voice was used for the recording, had asked London Transport if they would provide her with a CD of the recording, so that she could hear her husband’s voice as a reminder of their life together. Not only did London Transport oblige but they also reinstated the recording at one of the stations that his wife regularly used, so that she could continue to hear his voice proclaiming the message "*mind the gap*".

It would do us no harm if we were each to hear those words whenever we find that our thoughts and circumstances are crowding us and controlling us. Words that remind us to be mindful of the gap, and to focus on the space between.

There is no one way to find or to enter into that gap. For each one of us it can be different and for each one of us there are a variety of methods that we can use. Simple breathing techniques, disciplined meditation practice, awareness, prayer, a walk in the woods or along the beach, inner-journeying, taking a bath, deep relaxation, all of these are valid tools and whichever method works for you is good. You also don't need to restrict yourself to just one. The important thing is to remember that they are only tools to experience Stillness, and are not, in themselves, the end goal or destination. It is possible to reach a point where we are not just using these tools to reach that state of Stillness, but we are actually living in the gap and being the observer of all our thoughts and activities. Watching every situation in our lives as it unfolds but not being controlled or smothered by those situations, events and thoughts.

Keep it simple. We don't need to make this into a chore or turn it into a difficult process. **Living and abiding in the Stillness** is as simple as breathing. Every morning when I wake up I find that my heart is beating, my blood is flowing around my veins, my lungs are taking in and then expelling air, all the organs in my body are doing the job that they have been designed to do. I don't have to remind myself to breathe; I don't have to kick-start my heart in order for it to begin pumping. Life, and all that is needed to maintain life, just happens. It just is. It is my belief that it is no different with our spiritual life. The problem lies with the fact that we have allowed our physical existence to take precedence over our spiritual existence.

So then, let's use the tools that we have available to allow us to make contact with our spiritual life, and bring us back to where that pure, divine energy which is our spirit, our real self, is restored to its rightful place of authority in our lives.

Don't misunderstand me here, I am not saying that the physical existence is not important, or is inferior in any way. It is important that we look after and care for our physical needs, as it is the physical that provides the vehicle for the spiritual to express itself in our human manifestation. It is however, the spirit that is the driver of the vehicle. It is the driver who controls the vehicle, not the vehicle that controls the driver.

Human beings are naturally sociable creatures. We are generally happier when we live in a community or society that we feel a part of, whether it is a city or a village. We find comfort and safety in being members of some form of social network be it actual or virtual, enjoying a sense of belonging. We love to communicate, we write letters or emails, talk on the phone or face to face, we send text messages, we interact with those in our circles and with those outside of our normal circles. Perhaps then it is for these reasons that we often find the concepts of silence and solitude uncomfortable or even frightening.

"*Silence is golden.*" Silence is not something to be afraid of or to feel uncomfortable with. Silence can be a refuge, a time when we can be in the space, a time when we can listen and hear. Without the silence, all is just noise. There is an incredible beauty in silence which is to be treasured in a modern world where to experience true silence is a rarity. As I sit writing these words I am coming to the end of a week's stay at a lovely old cottage in a place called Bontddu, right on the water's edge of the estuary near Dolgellau in North Wales. Each morning during my stay here I have been getting up early to spend some time writing before anyone else is around. As I spend some time in Stillness meditation, it is wonderful not to be disturbed by all the usual sounds of life, yet still there is not perfect silence. The ducks, gulls and herons make their occasional calls to each other, the blue tits, robins and other birds sing to welcome the morning, the water ripples as the tide draws it inland and then back towards the Irish Sea, the trees rustle in the wind, but at times like these it is so much easier to "hear" the space between the sounds and to be aware of one's own "being".

I love my bed. I always have done. As a child, each morning during term-time I would hear my mother calling up the stairs. *"Come on, get up! You'll be late for school!"* During the school holidays the words would change slightly, *"Come on, get up! You can't stay in bed all day!"* Even into adulthood, the prospect of having a lie in was something to relish. Staying in bed on a Sunday morning until it was nearly lunchtime, listening to *The Archers* and *Desert Island Discs* on the radio became almost a ritual. I don't know if it is an age thing or whether it is just a matter of "wising-up" to the realisation of how wonderful those morning hours are and how much can be done by enjoying the stillness of the hour, making one ready for the day ahead, but these days I actually find it hard to stay in bed once I am awake. If, like I used to, you find it hard to rise early, a great incentive is to keep the curtains at the bedroom window open at night, allowing you to wake up to gently changing light as each new dawn breaks. By making that early start, you are giving yourself the opportunity to experience and enjoy a measure of silence before the world around you kicks into action.

We've probably all been in situations when someone has felt the need to "break the silence" and words have been spoken simply because it was too quiet. In my book "*Be Still*", I recounted the incident of a diner who said nothing during a particular meal, he offered no words to the conversation that was taking place and when asked why he was so quiet, replied that if he didn't have anything worth saying, then he would say nothing. To be in the company of someone and to feel secure and safe enough to be silent in their presence is a thing to be treasured. There is not that sense of awkwardness when no one says anything, but rather a sense of peace and trust. I always used to be known as a talker, someone who could be relied upon to start a conversation, to express an opinion or to crack a joke to break the ice. Looking back now, I am aware that I have actually always been a shy person and this talkative side of me came out of a nervousness and a feeling of discomfort, a lack of self-esteem and awareness. I still behave like this from time to time but thankfully those times are becoming less frequent as I remind myself to hold back and **Be Still**, to allow the silence its space, to mind the gap.

Another thing that many people seem to be fearful of in this world of constant communication, is solitude. Solitude, like silence, is something to be embraced and treasured. I'm not suggesting that we all take to a monastic lifestyle or head off into the mountains to be hermits, but it is good to have time alone. Time away from all the trappings and demands of a technological world that means that we are constantly in touch with friends, family and business contacts through the many wireless devices we have at our disposal. Just try walking down any street in any town or city and count the number of people who can be seen either talking or sending messages via their mobile phones. As wonderful as these pieces of technology are, they can also hinder us from experiencing a sense of confidence in our self. Whilst allowing communication with the world, modern technology can also stand in the way of our ability to communicate with those close to us, as well as to our own self and the divine source within us.

It is so easy to allow our phones, laptops, notebooks etc., to control and dominate our lives. Imagine what it would be like, even if it was only for half an hour, to switch off all these devices - no phone, no Internet, nor radio or Television. Having disconnected from technical communication, imagine then how it would feel to take yourself away from other people so that there is no conversation, no distraction. Take yourself off into the woods or onto the beach. Maybe just go and sit in the garden or shut the door to a room in your house, put up a "do not disturb" sign and cut yourself off from everything that would distract you from being in your own company. It really is not difficult, but I'm sure that there are many people reading this now who are finding all sorts of excuses as to why they could not possibly do this. Let me tell you now, there is absolutely no reason why you cannot take 30 minutes out of your day to be in the presence of your inner self and away from all other communication. If your excuse is children or caring for elderly relatives, get up half an hour before they do, or wait until they are in bed and switch the Television off and forego the regular soap that you always watch. If your excuse is "work commitments" believe me, by taking time out for some solitude you will find that dealing with the pressures and tasks of your working life will become so much easier as in the **Stillness** you find inspiration and creativity. There really is nothing stopping you. No more excuses, **Be Still**.

14

STOP, LOOK, LISTEN

I'd like to ask you to make a regular practice, at least once a day and beginning when you come to the end of this particular chapter in the book, to take time to Stop, Look and Listen.

Whatever it is that you are doing at any time of the day that you choose, Stop. Put the book down. Pull the car over into a lay-by. Stop walking through the park and sit on a bench. Unplug the iron. Stop listening to the radio or the mp3 player. Put the pen down. At some point in the day, whatever it is that you are doing - just Stop.

Once you have stopped, I want you to look; to observe. There are so many things that you can learn just by observing the things that you can see, wherever you might be. Right now I am sitting in the sunroom of a holiday cottage I have been staying in all week. If I look out of the window I can see the rain falling and the drops hitting onto the surface of the river as it flows past on its journey towards the river mouth and into the sea.

I can also see, inside the room, piled up on a table in the corner, boxes of games that we have played during the evenings in the cottage. Scrabble, Othello, Memorise, Uno and quite a few others.

Now, having looked, take time to Listen. Listen to what your inner-voice, that spirit within is saying to you about what you see.

Looking at the rain I am being reminded that as each individual drop becomes one with the river and eventually one with the sea, until the warmth comes and the water evaporates and rises up to become one with the clouds, until the clouds break and the rain falls once again into the river. (See the meditation in my previous book, *"Be Still - Simple Keys to Living a Spiritual Life in a Material World."*)

As I look at the pile of games, I am aware that this is our last day here and soon we will be packing things away and moving on. The games are done with and we won't be needing them again, and so I start to think about the things in my life that are done with and that I won't ever need again. Events, people, dilemmas, puzzles. Things that can be put away as I move on, things that don't need to be left on show as they belong to a time that is past and not the now.

Wherever you find yourself as you stop, whatever it is that you see as you look and observe, there is always something that can be learnt. There is always some wisdom that can be gleaned. There is always some guidance to be received.

Stop, Look, Listen.

Do it now.

15

LET GO AND MANIFEST

Up until the last few years my relationship with money has never been particularly healthy. I had been led to believe that while some people were born to have wealth and riches, others, myself included, were born to struggle and be poor. My parents worked hard so that we never actually went without, but we also never had much of the luxuries of life - that was not for folk like us.

I was once told by a palmist that I would never have money and for many years after, she was proved right - because I believed her. I believed it was my lot to always have to count the pennies and to live with the aid of a credit card and bank loan. It took me a long time to come to the point of **realisation** that this was not the case and to experience what it was to live an abundant life. I came to understand that there is no difference between the wealthiest billionaire on the planet and me. We both come from the same source, we are both made up of the same energy, we are in fact "one". We all have the same access to the divine, limitless, universal Bank of Abundance in order to withdraw all that we require to fulfil our purpose in this incarnation. There is no need to need. The reality is, that not only are we all one with the creative energy of the universe, we are that creative energy and so we have the ability to create for ourselves, in order to be who and what we are meant to be.

People often ask me how I was able to manifest all that was needed to open The Centre, or how I was able to manifest the time and resources to write "*Be Still*", my first book. I firmly believe that life is simple but, for whatever reason, we just choose to make it complicated. The answer to how I was able to manifest the necessary time, money and resources is, like everything else, actually really simple - I stopped trying.

We waste so much energy and effort by trying to do things, by trying to force situations and make things happen too quickly rather than sitting back and allowing the divine flow of energy to take us with it. I don't mean we should sit back and do nothing, what I mean is that we should relax and trust in our intuition and listen to the Stillness within. When we relax and allow the universe to support us, to hold us up and to guide us, it is then that we start to see the opportunities unfold before us, along with the synchronicities of events that occur as we follow the path of the labyrinth. And when those opportunities unfold and the synchronicities happen we must be ready to act and to move and be willing to grasp with both hands all that is offered to us by the universe.

Music has always been a part of my life ever since I was a young child. My father had a good baritone voice and I remember that he would often sing hymns and Welsh songs, both at home and at special family occasions. Being brought up in a Salvation Army household, I learnt to read and play music from about the age of 7 and eventually went on to work as a professional musician for more than 25 years. My taste in music is very eclectic and over the years I have learnt to play a number of different instruments. I particularly remember a time when I decided that I would like to learn to play the bodhrán. The bodhrán is an Irish drum used in traditional Irish folk music, it looks a bit like a large tambourine but without the bells and is played by hitting the skin in a brush-like movement with a wooden beater. I spent many hours trying to master the technique and trying to get the rhythm transferred from my brain, down my arm and onto the skin of the drum. Let me tell you now that the bodhrán is not a particularly easy instrument to play, and the more I concentrated and tried, the harder it was to get the right movement and action in my wrist and hand. Then one day I stopped trying and relaxed, listening to the music and allowing myself to go into what can only be described as a hypnotic or meditative state, which in turn allowed the rhythm to flow through me. All that effort of trying had got me nowhere, but by letting go and allowing, I found that I was able to play with confidence and fluidity.

The same principle can be applied to manifesting whatever it is that we require to fulfill our dharma. You're probably familiar with the phrase, "*Let go and let god*". Once you are prepared to let go and allow the creative energy to flow through you, you will soon discover that you are able to direct that energy to create for yourself the necessary situations and resources to live your abundant life, and to bring into existence all things required to build your purpose. I have already mentioned in a previous chapter that Jesus was reported to have said, *"Seek first the kingdom of god and all these things shall be added unto you"*. He also said, *"the kingdom of heaven is within you"*. Instead of striving, instead of trying, instead of looking for solutions outside of ourselves, if we turn within and find the **Stillness** that is the divine source within ourselves, and rest in that stillness, we will find that we are able to manifest "all these things".

Letting go can mean releasing our hold on many different things; our beliefs, our fears, our dependencies, our ambitions, our desires. All these things can stand in the way of our ability to manifest what we really should be reaching for.

If you believe that you are not worthy or that you are not good enough, you are putting restrictions on your own possibilities in life. If you believe that it is wrong, or sinful to have abundance in your life, you are closing the door on a great storehouse of blessings that actually belong to you.

We are told so many things as we go through our lives that cause us to have a blinkered, limited vision of what life can be for us. Our parents, our schools, our religious leaders so very often plant into our minds reasons why we cannot or should not do things. If you want to live a complete and fulfilled life it is time to let go of these life-limiting beliefs and see that you are part of a bountiful universe with limitless possibilities.

If you have a fear of failing or of falling at the first hurdle, that fear can take over from your willingness to trust and to move forwards along your path to abundance. Let go of your fears and allow yourself to trust the voice of the stillness as it directs and guides you through your divine intuition.

Many of us rely on what we have known, the things that have made us feel safe. We depend on them even though they may be restricting us and holding us back. Just like I was with the swimming pool and the ice rink, never letting go of the bars at the edge, until we release our hold we can never fully experience and enjoy the freedom.

Sometimes it can be the case that our ambitions and desires are not in alignment with the spirit within, with the result that we either get stuck in the striving to achieve something that is not right for us, or we realise our goals but still we are left with a sense of dissatisfaction because it is not in line with our highest calling or purpose. These misdirected ambitions can also cause us to miss out on what we should really be journeying towards, and so not achieving the fullness and abundance that is possible for us.

So, we come back to the same thing, in order for us to know our purpose and then to manifest all that we require to fulfill that purpose, we must first let go of everything that might hinder us and hold us back. Then, letting go, we take time to **Be Still**, to enter the **Stillness** and to connect with the Stillness. It is in the Stillness that we have knowledge of our purpose and our role. It is when we **dwell in the Stillness** that our path is clear and simple and all that we need, and the means to manifest what we need, is provided for us.

16

ALL YOU NEED IS LOVE

As I go into the seventh decade of my life I am still learning about love. Over the years I have written songs about love, I've experienced love in various forms and degrees, I've thought a lot about love, I've longed for it at times and shied away from it at other times. Too often love is just a word that is used without a real appreciation of what it is or what it can be. It's hard to put love in a box and to actually say "this is what love is". The Greeks had different words to label different types of love and in this chapter I'd like to look at some of those different types as we move towards experiencing abundant love.

The first two types of love are very similar and known as Storge and Philia. In both ancient and modern Greek, Storge means affection. Philia, in modern Greek also describes affectionate love as well as friendship. A concept developed by Aristotle, it is the sort of love that embraces loyalty, both amongst family, friends and community as well as a love for an enjoyable activity. Storge would be used to describe the love that a parent has for a child.

The third type of love, Eros, covers such feelings as sensual desire, intimate and passionate love. It is deeper than the love of friendship. Plato also described it as being an appreciation of beauty, including the beauty within the person who is loved so that it wasn't necessarily to do with physical attraction, which is how we have come to understand "platonic relationships".

The fourth Greek word to describe a type of love is

Agápe. Agápe can be described as “divine love”, it is both unconditional and sacrificial, the deepest of love.

We considered before that we are one with the divine source, with spirit, with god. That being the case, try saying these words to yourself.

“God is love. I am god. Therefore I am love.”

As we make that connection with the divine stillness within and abide in that stillness, so we begin to manifest love in all areas of our lives. The love we begin to manifest is Agápe love. There is no expectation with this love; we offer it without any need of return, without any requirement. We share this love purely because it is our divine nature - it is what we do. A sure sign of a person’s state of enlightenment is the freedom with which they love.

Divine love has no limits, no boundaries. It is for all people, all things, all of creation, and it asks for nothing in return. The image of god that has been portrayed through the ages by our religious institutions has often been that of one who offers love but demands something in return. A god that demands worship, obedience, sacrifice, servitude, and repentance is a false god. A god that makes demands of any sort is not a god of love. The idea that a loving father would condemn his children to an eternity locked away in a burning hell for not conforming to his will is abhorrent. Any human father who treated his children in such a way would be on a charge of child abuse and would spend a long time locked up themselves. Such a god does not exist.

True love is not judgmental, it is not jealous, it is all encompassing, it is pure and it is given freely. By acknowledging the connection to the divine stillness within, we also recognise that we are one with this divine, agápe love that we can allow to flow through us. In the stillness, examine your heart and ask yourself some simple questions about love.

"Do I expect anything in return for the love I give to my partner, my children, my friends?"

"Is my love given freely, without any ulterior motive?"

"Would it matter if my love was not returned?"

"Am I loving from a place of ego or from pure, divine love?"

"Do I love because I want to be loved?"

"Am I happy to keep giving love from that deep well of agápe *love which is within me?"*

An important aspect of this love is forgiveness. Blaming others, and blaming ourselves, is a strong barrier between living a mundane life and a life of abundance. Blame is a barrier that inhibits the flow of creative source energy in our lives, a dam that needs to be blown away by the power of love in order to allow the river of abundant life to flow. Once we can dispense with blame and know the joy of forgiveness, then we can experience more of the abundance and fullness of life.

I always find it deeply moving when I hear of someone who, being a victim of a crime is able to forgive the perpetrator of that criminal act. Or the parent of a child or partner of a loved one whose life has been taken by another, saying that they can forgive the one who has deprived them of the one they love. This is truly an act of divine love.

It is often said that to truly love another one must learn to love themselves. This truth can also be applied to forgiveness; we need to start by forgiving ourselves. Think about all those things that you blame yourself for, things that maybe cause you to be ashamed. It doesn't matter how big or small they are, see them as stones and boulders that are forming a dam across a river. That dam needs to be dismantled so take each stone and say to it *"I forgive myself"*.

Say to yourself,

"I forgive myself for those harsh words. I forgive myself for neglecting my family and friends. I forgive myself for being too busy. I forgive myself for stealing, for hurting, for not showing consideration. I forgive my self for misleading and misrepresenting the facts.", whatever it is, allow yourself forgiveness. But don't just say the words, feel the forgiveness and then feel the sense of release as the river starts to flow more easily. Then, when you have forgiven yourself, turn your mind to those whom you need to forgive, those whom you blame for whatever reason. You don't even have to face that person, although that would hold even more power, you could just forgiven them in your own soul. Sometimes it isn't possible to come face to face with someone you need to forgive, they may have passed on, they may not even know that you are holding this blame towards them - it really doesn't matter, the important thing is that you dismantle this dam of blame that is restricting the flow.

Another, and possibly the most important, fact about forgiveness is that in so doing you are also helping to break down the dam that is hindering the other person from enjoying the flow of abundance. Remember, you are showing this love for both yourself and for others, not for what you will receive back, but simply because this love is your nature. The purpose of your giving is to give, not to get.

One final thing about forgiveness is that in reality, the only reason we need to forgive either others, or ourselves is because we have made a judgement that an action or a word was wrong. When we are truly experiencing the flow of agápe love through us forgiveness becomes something we never need to do, because we have not passed judgement, we have not appropriated blame, we have not condemned. Without that act of judgement there is no need to forgive.

If we can view love as the creative energy of the universe, or the nature of the divine source that we call god and to which we are inseparably connected, all we have to do is to **allow** that energy to continually flow through us.

17

SPECIAL GIFTS

You may have often heard it said that someone has a special gift to be able to heal, or to use their psychic abilities. I want to tell you now that nobody has a "special" gift. There is nothing in the nature of god that you cannot do.

The divine source of the universe is limitless, it knows no restrictions. You came from that source, you are part of that source, and you share the nature of that source. Nobody is naturally more connected to that source than you are.

When a small child falls over and hurts his knee, he runs straight to his mother and mother rubs or kisses the knee better. The pain recedes as the child relaxes and feels safe in the arms of the one who loves him. The mother never had to go on any healing course to learn how to do this, it just comes naturally out of love and connection to the divine nature – even if the mother is not aware of her source.

It is no special gift, we all have the ability to heal and to be healed when we allow the source energy to flow through us.

There are those who are considered to be gifted in manifesting material blessings and seeing all their physical needs and desires being met. The same principle applies here; we are all part of and connected to the creative energy that has manifested everything that is, and as such we are also able to manifest those things that we need in order to fulfill our purpose, to **realise** our dharma in this incarnation. Allow yourself to be totally immersed in the divine spirit and you will see the miraculous become the norm.

Others are considered to be gifted in being able to communicate with the spirit world, to receive messages from those who do not possess a physical body or who have passed on to another life. Exactly the same principle applies here, this is not some kind of special gift. The idea of special gifts implies that some are more worthy to receive these so-called gifts, or that they have been shown some sort of favouritism in being chosen, or that they are in some way better than others.

Every one of us, no matter who we are, is able to communicate with spirit because **we are spirit**. It doesn't take any special gift; you don't need an intermediary to make contact for you, you are spirit and by **realising your spiritual nature** you can move into the spiritual realm whenever you want to.

I have written before about those who I feel trivialise and misuse this ability. It is my belief that the reason we have those that we call mediums and spiritualist groups and churches is because the majority of us are not aware that as spirits we are connected to every other spirit and as such can commune with them at will. Amongst those whom I count as some of my closest friends and acquaintances are a number of practicing mediums, and in no way do I want to belittle their work or abilities. They perform a service to those who have not yet **realised** their unlimited nature and need that reassurance that the medium brings.

Before I introduce you to a simple meditation technique that will help you to commune with the spirit world I feel that I should point out that, in my opinion, it is not necessarily helpful, or even spiritually healthy to keep trying to make contact with those who have passed on from this life. It is my belief that this can tie down the spirit of the loved one and hold them back from moving forwards in their new life or incarnation. Once my time in this body is over I am going to be ready to move forwards to whatever is in store for me next.

When we are in spirit we have no thought for our selves, there is no ego and no wanting. With that in mind it is quite possible that the spirit of a loved one will hang around for as long as we hold on to them, but I honestly feel that for us to keep calling and holding on to them is something that comes from a selfish motive and is actually holding back the progress of the departed spirit.

However, I do believe there are times when it is important for us to be able to contact those who have gone before in order for us to tell them something, rather than for them to tell us something. We may need to ask forgiveness for something that was left undone. We may need to give forgiveness in order to bring freedom for ourselves or for the departed. We may just simply need to say something that was left unsaid, to say *"I love you"* because we neglected to do so when we had the chance.

When we go into a deep meditation we are entering into the realm of spirit, we are **realising** our connection with our source, and we are going to that place from which we all came and to which we will all return when our life in this physical incarnation is over. It is in that place where we can meet with and talk to those who have gone before.

When you meditate allow yourself to physically relax and allow your mind to become still. At first you will be aware of your surroundings and your thoughts as they pass through your mind, but allow them to do just that – to pass through. Don't dwell on your thoughts, acknowledge them and then let them go. This may take some time at first but don't worry and don't get stressed about it. It often helps to focus on your breathing, counting each breath as it comes in and as it goes out. By focusing on your breathing, each time a thought grabs your attention and you find yourself getting lost in it, draw your focus back to your breathing. Continue to do this each time you drift away with your thoughts, and as you do so you will experience the stillness in your mind and in your body. Don't try to stop thinking, rather learn to control your thinking.

Control your thinking by imagining that you are in a beautiful place where you feel calm and relaxed, warm and peaceful. Allow your imagination to explore this place, feeling the textures, smelling the aromas, seeing the colours and taking in all that is around you. When you feel settled and comfortable in this place, imagine perhaps a door or a particular tree or stone, maybe a park bench where you are going to have your meeting with whomever it is that you wish to commune. In your imagination, make your way to this place, sit down or open the door, whatever it is that you need to do and picture the person as you remember them – they are there in this place of spirit for you to spend time with them and to say the things that you feel you need to say. Enjoy the few moments that you have together, you may find that they have words to share with you, it may be that they just listen to what you have to say. The important thing is that you have entered into the realm of spirit and they are there in spirit with you, so treasure the moment with love. Once you have said what you have to say, show your gratitude to them and release them so that they can continue on their eternal journey, before you come back to continue on your physical journey.

An important thing to understand here is that in the realm of spirit there is no time, unlike in the material world. So, no matter how long it may have been since the person passed over from this life, in that place of timeless eternity you will always be able to find them, and you don't need to have any special gift to be able to do so.

PART TWO

INSPIRATION

From time to time I write and post my thoughts on the **Be Still** Facebook page and on my on-line blog. Sometimes it may be just a single sentence or a few lines, sometimes a few paragraphs, depending on what I feel inspired to write. What follows on the remaining pages is a selection of those writings, published together for the first time. Some of the writings appear as they were originally presented, others have been edited and/or added to.

1

ACCEPTANCE AND SURRENDER

What do we normally do when we are faced with problems and difficulties in our lives? When obstacles and challenges confront us? When we encounter financial or health problems? The physiological reaction that occurs in response to a situation that we perceive to be threatening or harmful in any way, is commonly known as the "fight or flight" response. We either step into a confrontational mode or we run away from the situation.

A person who gets into difficulties in deep water and starts to struggle and fight is more likely to end up drowning; but one who surrenders to the flow has a chance of being taken to safety.

Accepting whatever situation you may find yourself in is not always easy, but, having the willingness and ability to surrender to that situation, means that you are able to rise above your circumstances and rest in the knowledge that all things actually work together for your good when you are coming from a place of connection with your source. It may not be easy to see it at the time, but when we do rise above the situation we are in, we are able to see it more clearly and with greater understanding and awareness.

Imagine that you are standing at the side of the road when a big parade is passing by. First of all you see the marching band going past, followed by the drum majorettes, after them you see the carnival queen passing the spot where you are standing and then more bands and floats as the parade continues to make its way down the road. And as you stand there and see the parade passing before your eyes, you can be forgiven for thinking that it is all happening in linear time. However, if you were to view the parade from a helicopter high above the marching bands and floats, you would see it all, from beginning to end in one instant. It is a matter of perspective. When we view things from a mundane, base level we see it in terms of past, present and future. But when we rise above the mundane we can see that all things are happening now and that now is the only time that is.

The problems that you may be facing, the illness that you may be experiencing, the bills that are piling up, are all just small parts of the parade that is your life. Coming into conflict with what is happening in your life is not the answer. Running away from the circumstances you find yourself in will not change those circumstances. Acknowledging them, accepting them and surrendering to them, enables you to rise above them and to see them for what they actually are - a part of your life's parade.

How many times have you heard, or even said, in reply to the question "*How are you?*" the words "I'm *alright, under the circumstances*"? How sad is that position? Who on earth would choose to be *under* the circumstances?. **Be Still** and rise above your circumstances and view them from a higher vantage point.

2

MEDITATION

One of the most common misconceptions that people often have about meditation is that they believe they need to empty their minds and be clear of any thoughts. This really is not the case and such a concept can actually turn people away from meditating, as they find this so difficult to do.

Meditation is about connecting with the source energy, divine mind, spirit within, god - whatever term one chooses to use to describe the pure energy that is within each one of us. This doesn't mean that we have to empty our mind of all thoughts; in fact it means pretty much the opposite. Rather than having no thought, when we meditate we actually have control over our thoughts so that they come into alignment with the source energy and our thoughts become what I call "god-thoughts".

One of the biggest stumbling blocks that people encounter when it comes to meditation is that of unwelcome, lingering thoughts. I've lost count of the number of times that I have heard someone say that they have tried meditating but have given up because they have been unable to blank their minds and stop themselves being bombarded by random and irrelevant thoughts. Let me tell you now that you will never stop thoughts coming into your head, I'm sorry but that is just the truth of it. The secret is, not to hold onto those thoughts. The discipline of meditation comes, not in clearing your mind but in cleaning your mind. Start to think those things that are pure, good, right, healthy, positive etc., and don't hold on to thoughts that are negative, critical or judgmental. Think as "god" would think, this is true meditation.

It is when we allow our thoughts to be in alignment with the divine energy that we gain clarity and understanding, answers and direction.

A simple technique for meditation that works for both the beginner and the experienced practitioner alike, is to focus your thoughts on your breath. Actually feel and experience each breath as it goes up into your nose and then as it goes down and out of your nose. To help concentrate on your breathing you may find it helpful to count the breaths or to visualise the air travelling up the nostrils and then down again. Don't rush it, take your time, and breathe slowly and deliberately. You are going to find that you are distracted by thoughts coming in, but don't let that discourage you. When that happens, simply draw your attention back to your breathing, counting the breath in and out. You might like to say in your mind the words "*I breathe in . . . I breathe out*", or some variation of those words, whatever feels comfortable for you.

Everybody's experience is different, but the important thing is to keep returning to an awareness of your breathing. When we take deep breaths we allow ourselves to be still and to eliminate or shut out all the negative and irrelevant thoughts that come into our minds. One should acknowledge the unpleasant feelings one might have and say "*ok, I know that you are there but the past is over and done with, I am now living in THIS moment and will not let my memories of the past or my concerns of the future stop me from experiencing this moment.*"

The more you practice this, the easier and more natural it will become for you.

And remember, you don't need to always be sitting down in a quiet place in order to meditate.

Meditation is a state of being rather than an action. Meditation is about **realising** your connection with the spirit within and the greater spirit of the universe, the source, that which we call god, and as such is something that can be experienced 24 hours a day, 7 days a week. Wherever you are, whatever you are doing you can draw your attention to your breathing and remind yourself of that connection. On my phone I have a "mindfulness bell" app, the sound of a singing bowl rings at random intervals to remind me to breathe, to relax, and to be aware of my spiritual connection. I never know when it is going to sound, I could be driving, writing, walking, ironing a shirt, listening to music or digging the garden, but when it rings it is that gentle reminder that I am part of the greater whole and I awaken my awareness.

A wonderful Tibetan Lama that I know, speaks about how some people set time aside to meditate and sit themselves stiff and upright, saying, "*ok, I have to meditate now, I must stop thinking about everything and spend the next 30 minutes meditating, even if it is uncomfortable for me I must meditate*", and the meditation becomes a chore, a stressful experience. After 30 minutes and the meditation time is over they can breathe again and relax. That type of meditation is not going to help anyone. The most beautiful meditation is when we are mindful and aware of our connection - whatever we are doing.

Meditation is not something that we should consider to be a challenge or a chore but it is actually our natural state as spiritual beings.

3

LET IT BE

It has been said many times that we are human beings not human doings. People's lives are often defined by what they "do", rather than who they are. Judgements are made, labels are allocated, and life-affecting decisions can all be influenced by what a person does. Throughout my life I have "done" many things and the things that I do have often changed. Many of the things that I did in my 20's I no longer do in my 60's. What I do is not who I am. Neither do I have to prove anything by "doing".

Fulfillment in life doesn't come from what I do but from who I am; not from doing but from being. "Being" doesn't mean that we stop "doing" and become inactive. If that were the case we would just sit around contemplating our navels and never getting anywhere. For me the concept of "being" means to be myself, not an idea of myself that others might want to see, or that I think others might want to see. And to be myself means that I recognise that I am actually connected to, and part of, the source of everything. When I allow myself to be in that place of stillness I realise and accept that the only time is "now". Not the past or the future, but now. In that space I know that there is nothing to be concerned about or worry about, and that makes me "feel" good, it makes me feel connected, it makes me feel like I am actually a part of the creative energy of the universe, so that nothing that needs to be done in my life is unachievable. It makes me feel that anything that I need in order to fulfill my purpose, I can manifest it, sometimes by taking opportunities, sometimes by using my creative energy, sometimes by just accepting what comes in my path.

The truth is that when I am comfortable in my "being" I am able to do things in a fulfilling and satisfying way.

Be Still and BE.

4

JUST FOR TODAY

. . . on your social networking site, only post or share the things that are positive and uplifting. Notice what a difference it will make to your news-feed if all your friends did the same. No more negativity, no more criticism, whether it is of other individuals, the government, religious institutions, the economy or even the weather. Give it a go JUST FOR TODAY, and if you like it and it makes you feel better, why not try it tomorrow as well.

5

STRONGER THAN THE DARKNESS

If where you are today there are a lot of clouds, remember that the sun is still shining behind them.

Before too long the clouds will disperse and the warmth and light of the sun will shine through again.

Remember that whenever you experience clouds in the future, the sun will still be there waiting to break through once more.

The light is always stronger than the darkness.

Imagine that you have before you two sealed boxes - one containing total darkness and one containing pure light - when you open them both to reveal the contents all you will see is the light.

6

ACCEPTANCE

Have you noticed that sometimes people who profess to have a level of spirituality and to walk a spiritual path, see no problem in ridiculing and negatively criticising the beliefs of others. An attitude that comes across as arrogant and superior, lacking in love, tolerance and understanding.

We do not all have the same belief, we do not all walk the same path, but it is my belief (and yes, I accept that I may be wrong. It's just what I happen to believe) that we are all one and we are all part of the same universal consciousness.

The one who believes that their way is the right way and that all other ways are mistaken or wrong is pretty sure to be deceiving themselves and to be in danger of deceiving others as well.

The law of attraction would say that by giving respect we attract respect. Similarly, if we show a lack of respect and tolerance then we are inviting the same to our own lives.

Today, show respect and tolerance - even if we don't share agreement. You never know, by listening and being open, we may learn things that might cause us to view things differently.

7

LET YOUR LIGHT SHINE

Driving through the beautiful Carmarthenshire countryside this morning, with a fiery red sun rising in front of me, was just another reminder of how wonderful life is. It is all so easy to take things for granted, so try to remember to show gratitude for all that life has to offer and take a lesson from the sun. Let your light shine and just as that sun-rise made me feel good this morning so your light shining will help to make others feel good.

But don't forget what it is like to have been in the darkness for some time and the light is switched on, it takes a little while for the eyes to become accustomed to the light, but once the eyes become adjusted and focused, everything becomes clear. So don't worry about your light being too bright for some people - when they are ready they will see clearly.

8

HERE TO BE

We are not here to make other people see our point of view. We are not here to make other people believe what we believe. We are not here to force or to convert. We are simply here to be who we are. That is our dharma, our purpose - to simply "be". By simply "being" we are helping to make the world the perfect place that it really is.

9

BETTER THAN YESTERDAY

We don't need to be better than anyone else, we don't need to be more spiritual than anyone else - in fact we don't even need to compare ourselves with anyone else. The only thing we need to aim for each day is to be better than we were the day before.

10

THE TRUTH IS . . .

We have all the answers to all of our questions and problems. Connect with the **Stillness** within and listen.

The truth is not "out there", it is within you and the truth will set you free.

In whatever you are doing, **Be Still,** tune in to your inner stillness and follow your heart and your soul.

11

LIFE'S JOURNEY

When we set out on any journey, we are travelling from one place to another. When we get to our destination we can take a rest, we can feel satisfied with a sense of accomplishment, we can celebrate the fact that we have reached our goal. We can look forward to being in a new place with all the excitement and possibilities that may be offered.

Our life is a journey and we need not fear reaching its end - it is why we are on the journey, in order to get to our destination.

Enjoy the journey and all that you experience along the way, and know that when you reach the end of your travelling there will still be many unknown and exciting discoveries to be made.

12

AT THE START OF THE DAY

If you are one of those people who find mornings difficult, try coming at them from a different direction. Before you get out of bed, spend a couple of minutes reminding yourself and thinking about all the things you have to be grateful for. Make a mental list, it can be anything - your bed, your home, your family, the fact that you are alive, the opportunities that lie ahead - the list may well be a lot longer than you first imagine.

When you've made your list, wrap it in love and gratitude and be ready to face the morning with joy and a smile.

13

WE CAN CHANGE THE WORLD

I have been thinking about something that a friend said to me recently about climate change. They said, "*global warming is part of our journey. It will be interesting to see how we, and it, unfold. How we adapt, learn and continue living*".

The danger with simply accepting things as part of our journey is that we can become fatalistic and just sit back and do nothing. If we are all connected to each other and to the creative energy of the universe, which is basically "love", then it is our responsibility to extend that love to all of creation.

Part of our purpose, our dharma, is to show love to all people and to the planet on which we live. If we view such things as climate change, poverty, violence, war - things that destroy life – as, "*that's just the way it is and it's part of our journey*", then we are neglecting and turning our backs on our responsibility.

It is right to say that we are spiritual beings having a physical experience, but the truth is that we are in this physical experience for a reason, and with that comes responsibility. I often say that sometimes we can be so spiritually minded that we are no earthly use.

The same principle can be applied to our view of karma. If taken to an extreme and we believe that everything that happens, good or bad, is because it is a result of karma - we can sit back and allow the planet to be destroyed, people to be killed, people to be raped, millions to starve because it is all part of their karma. This is to totally misunderstand the divine mind and our reason for being on this planet. Karma is not about judgement and retribution, it is simply cause and effect. You are reading this book because either you bought it or somebody gave it to you, and that was because it was on sale somewhere, in a shop or at an event or online. The book was there because a while back I decided to write it. I decided to write it because of experiences and inspirations that I have had. I had those experiences and inspired thoughts because I exist. I exist because one day my parents fell in love. The be-causes can continue as far back as the beginning of the universe. That, my friend is cause and effect; that is karma.

We all have a responsibility to allow divine, unconditional love to flow through us and to make a positive difference - not just sit back and let everything pan out.

One person may not be able to change the whole world, but if each one of us does something to change our own world, the world that is immediately around us, then we will see that the whole world can be changed.

Today, and every day, determine to make a difference.

14

FINDING ONE'S SELF

My teenage years were spent during the mid to late 1960s and the early 70s, a time when the world was changing. In the words of the musical "*Hair*" this was the "*dawning of the Age of Aquarius*". Many young people, and some not so young, set out on a journey of discovery, on a mission to "find themselves". Some headed off on physical journeys to spiritual centres around the world - to India, Tibet, Assisi. Today, there are still many who tread the same path while others stay closer to home and visit places such as Glastonbury, Findhorn or Iona. These pilgrimages may help to a point and provide inspiration and edification, but the truth is that the only place you are actually going to find your true self is where you are, right here, right now, within your self.

Wherever you are, whether it is at home or at work, in the city or in the mountains of the Himalayas, **Be Still** and look inside, for it is only there that you will find peace.

Only there, in the **Stillness**, will you find yourself.

It is only there in that quiet, sacred space in your soul that you will find the divine, whether you call it god, spirit, source, the divine mind, the creative life-force. . .

It is within each one of us.

It is within you.

Whatever sense of self or belonging, peace or spiritual

wholeness you are looking for - if you can't find it within yourself, you will never find it on the outside. All the travelling and pilgrimages to sacred sites and mystical lands will be of no use if you don't open the door to your inner heart and listen to the spirit within.

You can be sure that once you have found within, that which you are searching for, you will be conscious of it everywhere and in everything.

15

THE BLESSING OF GIVING

Whatever you think your needs are today, whatever you think is lacking in your life - just put all thoughts of it aside and focus on giving rather than getting. It is in giving that we actually **realise** how much we already have.

16

THE JOYS OF SPRING

As I write this, the sun is shining, the spring flowers in the garden are just about to open and the world is full of promise.

Whatever darkness we go through in our lives, the light is always able to shine through and dispel the darkness.

When things appear to be dormant, the promise of new life is just below the surface.

May your today be better than yesterday, and may your life be better everyday.

17

SEIZE THE DAY

Each day has its own opportunities. Don't come to the end of the day and say, "*I wish I'd done this*", or "*if only I'd done that*". Today only happens once so take the opportunities as they are offered. As you live in stillness, and connected to your source, you will have discernment to know which opportunities are for your benefit. Live each day with gratitude and receptivity, and then, when your days are coming to an end, you won't have to look back with regret.

18

THE POSITIVE/NEGATIVE BALANCE

A lot of emphasis is put on the power of positive thinking, something that I totally believe in. When we focus on the positive we are able to add energy to that and to bring about the manifestation or **realisation** of those thoughts. The same is true with regards to focusing on the negative, when we dwell on negativity we are again adding energy to the negative and bringing about an end-result that proves that what we were spending all our time worrying about, has actually happened. Focusing on the positive is indeed a good way to live.

However, as with so many things there is the danger of taking it to the extreme, an extreme that says we should never even think about the negative, we shouldn't consider what might go wrong or what pitfalls might be along the path. This kind of thinking can result in feelings of guilt and beating ourselves up when we do think about the negative. I want to make it clear here that thinking about the negative possibilities, and thinking negatively, are two entirely different things.

Thinking about the negative possibilities is an essential part of life, enabling one to be prepared and ready to deal with problems that might arise. Whenever I get into my car to take a journey it is imperative that I look ahead and make myself aware of any possible hazards or dangers, always being alert and ready to take action if required. It would be wrong of me to be in charge of a vehicle without any preparation or road-awareness. It would not only be potentially harmful for me but I would also be a potential danger to other road-users and pedestrians.

When an architect is designing any sort of structure he needs to be aware of possible dangers or influences that might affect the structure - the weight bearing load of a bridge, the ability of a tower-block to stand up against high winds, the drainage facilities and angles of the roof to protect against the weather, the siting of the building to withstand threats of flooding. All these things need to be taken into consideration. It is no use the architect designing and building the house whilst saying that he just needs to be positive and none of these things will ever happen.

The old boy-scout motto *"Be Prepared",* is far from being negative thinking, on the contrary preparedness is positive. Being aware of potential dangers or possible risks puts one in a positive position to face whatever may arise. It doesn't mean that you are expecting that the worst will happen, it means that you are ready should something go wrong. That's the difference between being aware of negative things and dwelling on them.

Be aware of the rocks on the path so that you can step over them.

19

CREATE YOUR OWN ABUNDANCE

As we are connected to, and part of, the creative energy of the universe, that same powerful creative energy is flowing through us.

This means that we are constantly creating our lives.

Understand the magnificence of this. By being still and **realising** our connection with the divine mind we can know our purpose and create all that we need to fulfil that purpose. **There is absolutely no reason for us not to live a fulfilled life**.

Create your perfect life today and don't put any limitations on your creativity.

20

BEYOND LIMITATION

Science tells us that energy constantly flows around and part of it may become matter at some time. Later it goes back into energy.

We, as humans, are made of pure energy. Before we manifest a physical existence we are energy, when our physical existence ends we continue as energy. We are all part of, and one with, the divine creative energy of the universe and as such, limits or barriers do not confine us.

As we **realise** our connection with the one energy that we are part of, we also **realise** that there is no limit to what we can achieve - we need not need.

Everything that is required for us to fulfil our purpose and dharma is already ours through this energy. This energy is love.

Do not limit yourself today - live in abundance and prosper in all that you do as you immerse yourself in the energy that you are.

21

THE REAL THING

When you strip away all the things that you think define you, you will finally come to your self.

When you break free from, and put aside all your attachments, be they physical, emotional, mental or even spiritual, the only thing you are left with is your self.

Understand that all these attachments only serve to create an illusion of who you are. An illusion that you believe to be you. An illusion that others, who observe you, believe to be you. This is not the real you, the real "I am".

Peel away those outer layers of illusion until you come to your self - the reality, the truth.

Know the truth and the truth will set you free to be who you really are.

22

BE(A)WARE

Awareness is about living in the “now”.

It is about accepting and appreciating what “is”.

To live in the moment means that the end result or goal is not your primary purpose for what you are now doing.

Take joy and satisfaction from the fact that you are experiencing each moment as it happens.

If your mind is only set on the destination, the pleasures and joy of the journey will pass you by and you will have missed something special.

Right now I am focused on, and being fulfilled by, the fact that I am typing out these letters which are forming these words. In so doing I am experiencing a vibrant awareness of being alive.

Whatever you are doing, at all times of the day, be focused and aware and know fulfillment.

23

IN THE SILENCE

So much can be gained with regards to our awareness and spiritual growth if we take time out to be silent and on our own. With no physical or material distractions we allow ourselves the space to listen to the inner-voice, the spirit, speaking.

Now, I know that it is easy to make all sorts of excuses as to why we neglect to find this space - time, commitments, family etc., but all it takes is to maybe get up half an hour earlier, before the rest of the household, or switch off the TV or radio for a while. Find a quiet room, take a bath, or go for a walk on the beach or in the woods or park. It doesn't even have to be for half an hour, 5 or 10 minutes will do. You could even shut yourself away in the bathroom or garden shed.

In the Stillness of silence and solitude, focus on your breathing and allow yourself to "be".

Find time today to **listen to the silence**.

24

KNOW YOUR TREASURE

Jesus is reported to have said the words, "*Where your treasure is, so will your heart be also.*"

What is it that you value the most?

Is your treasure that which is temporal? That which will pass away or decay?

Or is your treasure, the thing that you value the most; timeless, eternal, incorruptible?

If our heart and treasure is in our possessions, our relationships, our health, our career - all these things will pass away.

If our heart and the thing that we value the most is in that deep sense of being, the spiritual, our connection to the source of all that is, then we are truly experiencing fullness and eternal life. And, the wonderful thing is, we don't need an intermediary to make that connection - we are already one with that source.

25

LET IT GROW

Have you noticed how often we talk about growth as something we can make happen? Governments constantly talk about taking different measures to make the economy grow. We tell our children to "*grow up*!" as if it is something they can do by effort. The food industry wants to force growth by genetic modification. The farming world fattens up cattle by pumping them with growth hormones. Even in the world of spiritually-aware people there is a desire to stimulate growth by our practices.

The fact is that true growth happens naturally and without effort.

Have you ever tried sitting looking at a tree to watch it grow? You are not going to see much happening. The growth is slow and effortless and cannot be viewed with the naked eye, but when you revisit the tree after a matter of time you can see that growth has taken place. A couple of days ago I looked at the fruit trees in my garden and they were just beginning to show signs of buds appearing on the branches. Today, I went into the garden and those same branches are adorned with the colourful blossoms that appeared when I wasn't looking.

Those trees haven't been doing anything to force that growth, they haven't been stressing or striving in order to produce the blossom. They haven't been caught up with thoughts about needing to grow and how they can make it happen. They haven't been moving and running around the garden to find the best place to catch the sun, or a new source of life-giving energy. They have just been standing there in stillness and the growth has happened.

When we get concerned about our spiritual growth and try to speed it up in all manner of ways, we are actually behaving in the same way as those who are trying to genetically modify our crops. Growth comes about by **allowing**. We allow our roots to feed on the goodness and nutrients of the earth - the things that we learn from being in the present, from experiencing the now, and we also allow the light to shine on our leaves and branches, illuminating and energising us.

To paraphrase some wise words from Jesus:

"Who, by stressing can add growth to their life? Observe the flowers in the fields - they grow, without working at growth, yet even the richest man with all that he has, cannot be compared to their beauty."

Be Still, enjoy the present moment - embrace it, rest in it, allow the growth to happen.

26

FOCUS ON THE MOMENT

When we are focusing our attention on what we want to be, or what we want to have in the future, we are missing out on appreciating what we are now and what we have at this moment.

Each moment is unique and precious and so much joy can be had, by being mindful of who you are, where you are what you are doing in each moment.

In the **Stillness** of **realisation** and **mindfulness** is **fulfilment**.

For each moment you **are** all you need to be.

For each moment you **have** all that you need to be in that moment.

Be Still and be whole.

27

SEED GROWTH

A few months back, Kiera and I spent some time in the greenhouse and potting shed, sowing seeds ready to put into the vegetable plot. After a while we were eventually able to plant them out into the garden or into larger pots in the greenhouse.

During the last couple of weeks we have been starting to harvest the fruits of our initial sowing and recent meals have consisted mainly of vegetables and fruit that have come from our own garden.

So, what am I learning from this?

I'm learning that the seeds that I sow in every area of my life don't come to fruition overnight. Sometimes those ideas that we have and set in motion need to be left to germinate and to sprout before we can see them grow and reach maturity. This is not a matter of "being patient", rather it is about knowing and trusting that once the seed has been sown I can get on with the other things in life. I might have to re-visit and add some water to them when they need it. I might need to remove any weeds that would crowd them out or hinder their growth, but basically I just need to allow the soil, the sun and the rain to do what is natural.

The Universe ensures that those seeds that are sown in love and in the place where the ground is ready, will flourish and come to fruition.

Be Still and allow the creative energy of the universe to do what it does.

AFTERWORD

At the beginning of this book we looked at what I called The Tripod Effect and I set you a little task to see how balanced your life was between the material/physical, the emotional/mental and the spiritual. I'd like you, as we come to the final pages, to repeat the exercise and compare the tripod now with how it was at the beginning. If you have an actual tripod with a camera, take another photograph and compare it with the one you took originally.

Hopefully, as you are **realising** what you know and what you are learning, you are already starting to see that your life is more balanced and that you are seeing things more clearly and in focus.

Blessings to you on your way and may you go on and continue to enjoy a life of abundance and fulfilment.

Namaste

Don't allow your life to be affected by the external,
allow your life to affect that which is around you.

Jim Fox

ACKNOWLEDGMENTS

There are so many people who have been an inspiration to me throughout my life, and so many who continue to teach and inspire, and others who have been a wonderful support to me. My gratitude goes out to them all.

Amongst them I would particularly like to thank my brother Graham Reeves who has always been there for me throughout my life.

Once again my appreciation and thanks to my wife Kiera, and also to Mary Jones. Both of them made invaluable contributions to the finished work by reading, editing, and correcting my grammar.

*

IF WE ARE FACING IN THE RIGHT DIRECTION, ALL WE HAVE TO DO IS KEEP ON WALKING

Jim Fox *is an inspirational writer and speaker, based in South Wales. After spending many years as a professional musician, performing throughout the UK and Scandinavia, he trained as a Sound Therapist and, together with his wife, he runs an Holistic Centre, providing various therapies and training & workshop facilities, including offering free support and therapies to those living with cancer and other life-limiting conditions.*

By purchasing this book you have helped to ensure the continuation of this work – Thank you.

www.jimfox.info

www.thecentre-swansea.co.uk

Also available

Be Still

Simple Keys to Living A Spiritual Life in a Material World

by

Jim Fox

Published by
The Centre of The Labyrinth

ISBN 978-0-9573855-0-4

www.ingramcontent.com/pod-product-compliance
Ingram Content Group UK Ltd.
Pitfield, Milton Keynes, MK11 3LW, UK
UKHW021051200726
13857UKWH00003B/892